"Let's face it, the statistics are not good about grownups, especially men, and their ability to maintain close friendships outside their family. Bryan Loritts confronts this reality with a book-length antidote to a growing culture of friendless lives. His blunt honesty, practical remedy, biblical fidelity, and heart of charity will leave you hopeful that indeed, friendships new and old can endure."

Barry H. Corey, president of Biola University and author of *Love Kindness: Discovering the Power of a Forgotten Christian Virtue*

"Friendships are difficult to navigate; friendships among believers in Christ are no less difficult. They may even be more difficult as there is a level of accountability built into that friendship based on a mutual desire to live out the mandate to be like Christ. Dr. Loritts masterfully and lovingly leads us by way of careful exegesis through the powerful letter of Paul to Philemon. I highly recommend this book for anyone who wants to strengthen a friendship or repair a ruptured one."

Jody Moore, lead pastor of Transformation Church IE in Chino, California

"So much of friendship today is conditional and about convenience. Because it's guided by a fresh look at the New Testament and illustrated by his own raw friendship journeys, Bryan Loritts's book offers a compelling vision of friendship that's both attainable and worth sacrificing for."

Kara Powell, professor of youth and family ministry at Fuller Theological Seminary and coauthor of *Faith Beyond Youth Group*

"Bryan Loritts is an expert communicator. I have known Bryan for years, colabored with him, and been changed by his teaching. I believe the biblical insights shared in *Enduring Friendship* may be the most challenging, anointed, and transformative he's ever produced, and I have been waiting with great expectation for how the Lord will use this for his glory in his kingdom. This is the greatest work on reconciliation from a biblical worldview I have ever read!"

Vance Pitman, president of the Send Network and founding pastor of Hope Church Las Vegas

"Here's the truth: what you hold in your hands can transform your life. But let me warn you, this isn't the kind of book you read once and cross off the list. No, this book will bore into your very being and invite you into the depth of what true biblical friendship looks like. Loritts leverages the New Testament book of Philemon as his resource to challenge you to be a better friend. So buckle up and get ready to read the best book I've ever read on friendship."

Bobby Conway, author, pastor, and radio host

"One of my deepest desires is for real, engaging, lifelong friendship. Bryan Loritts once again provides the church with a timely book on a neglected subject of critical importance, written in his characteristically engaging, easy, entertaining-while-challenging way. We know what a marriage commitment looks like—what commitment does friendship desire? Bryan shows us how we can go from 'I will' at the beginning to 'I did' at the end of our days. I've seen Bryan up close enough to see how he lives these things out. This is a book that every Christian should read, implement, and pass on."

J.D. Greear, pastor of the Summit Church in Raleigh-Durham, North Carolina

"*Enduring Friendship* shatters the myth that friendship is little more than a casual relationship. Using his own experience and the apostle Paul's letter to Philemon as his framework, Bryan Loritts shows that friendships have the potential to enhance our gospel witness to the world as they demonstrate truth, repentance, and grace. At a time when true friendships are being replaced by shallow connections, the world needs this book. I need this book!"

Stan Jantz, chief executive officer of the Come and See Foundation

"In a world where we are seemingly more connected than ever, our personal relationships can often feel shallow and distant without deliberate attention and willing vulnerability. Bryan Loritts identifies the importance of deep and abiding friendship, and he tells us why it is worth the intentional effort to invest in the lives of others. *Enduring Friendship* is a wonderful encouragement to pursue God's good gift of human connection."

Amy Whitfield, executive director of communications for the Summit Church, Raleigh-Durham, North Carolina

ENDURING FRIENDSHIP

STICKING TOGETHER IN
AN AGE OF UNFRIENDING

BRYAN C. LORITTS

FOREWORD BY
JOHN MARK COMER

An imprint of InterVarsity Press
Downers Grove, Illinois

InterVarsity Press
P.O. Box 1400 | Downers Grove, IL 60515-1426
ivpress.com | email@ivpress.com

InterVarsity Press® is the publishing division of InterVarsity Christian Fellowship/USA®. For more information, visit intervarsity.org.

Scripture quotations, unless otherwise noted, are from The Holy Bible, English Standard Version, copyright © 2001 by Crossway Bibles, a division of Good News Publishers. Used by permission. All rights reserved.

While any stories in this book are true, some names and identifying information may have been changed to protect the privacy of individuals.

Published in association with the literary agency of Wolgemuth & Wilson.

The publisher cannot verify the accuracy or functionality of website URLs used in this book beyond the date of publication.

Cover design: David Fassett
Interior design: Jeanna Wiggins

ISBN 978-1-5140-0844-7 (print) | ISBN 978-1-5140-0846-1 (digital)

Printed in the United States of America ∞

Library of Congress Cataloging-in-Publication Data
Names: Loritts, Bryan C., author.
Title: Enduring friendship : sticking together in an age of unfriending /
    Bryan C. Loritts ; foreword by John Mark Comer.
Description: Downers Grove, IL : IVP, [2024] | Includes bibliographical
    references.
Identifiers: LCCN 2023038187 (print) | LCCN 2023038188 (ebook) | ISBN
    9781514008447 (print) | ISBN 9781514008454 (paperback) | ISBN
    9781514008461 (digital)
Subjects: LCSH: Friendship–Religious aspects–Christianity.
Classification: LCC BV4647.F7 L57 2024 (print) | LCC BV4647.F7 (ebook) |
    DDC 241/.6762–dc23/eng/20231017
LC record available at https://lccn.loc.gov/2023038187
LC ebook record available at https://lccn.loc.gov/2023038188

30   29   28   27   26   25   24 | 12   11   10   9   8   7   6   5   4   3   2   1

To my sons—
Quentin, Myles, and Jaden.

You're out of our home now,

and while I will always be Dad,

I hope to also be counted

among your friends.

CONTENTS

FOREWORD

John Mark Comer

Many years ago, I had the chance to travel to London with a few friends. We were there for a small gathering of pastors from around the world, and the first night, we borrowed from the local custom and went to the pub, naturally. At the far end of the table were four older men who had been close friends for almost forty years. They'd all come to faith together in the early '80s in South Africa and ended up planting churches all over the world. Yet they found a way to stay in relationship as the years passed. They would vacation together, travel to visit each other, call regularly. They had fallen out and reconciled, lived across the street from each other and lived across the world, officiated each other's kids' weddings and been at the funerals. They had traveled the Way together.

I have this very distinct memory of sitting at the other end of the table with my friends, all newer relationships, all of us young and untested. I remember watching the older men laughing, needling each other, making wildly inappropriate jokes for late-middle-aged pastors, telling story after story from their many years together.

And I remember leaning over to my friend Todd and saying, "Someday, I want *that*."

I did not grow up in a culture with any vision or example of long-term, "enduring" friendship, especially not for men. Friendship, sure. As long as it was seasonal and not too deep. But not *enduring* friendship. That day lifted the horizon of possibility over my life.

Drawing inspiration from that evening in the pub, I and a few others began to gather together a small band of men with the goal of lasting friendship: to walk together, spend time in community, share vulnerably, and go the distance.

I've been on this road of friendship for well over a decade. I'm still many years from my finish line, but this band of brothers has carried me farther than I ever hoped.

And yet, as Bryan writes, "The older I get, the more difficult friendship seems to be."

There's the one friend who ghosted me. He's cut off all relationship, and no matter how deep I pry, I can't get him to tell me what I've done. I'm left to speculate and live in loss . . .

The friend who slandered me and never apologized . . .

The one who stole from me . . .

It's been said our deepest wounds come from relationship, *but so does our deepest healing.*

In recent years, I've thought about giving up on long-term friendship altogether. Is it worth the pain? Do I keep walking through the valley, trusting that there are more mountains still to come? Or do I follow my primal instinct for self-preservation back into an isolated, individualistic mode of being?

Enter my friend Bryan's newest book. Bryan is painfully honest about the challenge of long-term friendships: "Soul-level friendship often feels like a full-time job with periods of bad compensation." Yet you read this book and come away burning with desire to bare your soul to another in love.

The only way I can make sense of this paradox is this: the throughline of this book is the gospel of Jesus. Bryan rightly teaches us that sin is "the problem with every relationship," and "sin is never just about the individual; it is also deeply relational." Hence, the only hope we have for enduring friendship is the gospel and grace of God.

I walked away from reading *Enduring Friendship* not only recaptured by the beauty of the gospel but also deeply moved by the power of grace. Bryan is a man who is enthralled by grace, steeped in grace, moved by it.

Bryan is a newer friend in my life. We've not walked enough road together to have any conflict or simmering tension, but if we continue a shared journey (and I very much hope we do), we inevitably *will*.

What then?

Then, grace.

Then we listen, forgive, let go, humble ourselves, take the place of a servant. We endure the only way possible: we model our friendship after the one who said, "I have called you friends."

Introduction

FROM "I WILL" TO "I DID"

When people get married, their bridesmaids and groomsmen stand with them saying, "I will." When people die, their pallbearers who carry them to the grave say, "I did." What a picture of friendship. It makes for a great card, but let's not kid ourselves: it's rare for someone to be carried to their final resting place by the same people who stood with them at their wedding.

Korie and I were wed on a July morning several decades ago. We were flanked on either side by men and women so dear that we asked them to stand with us as we exchanged vows, entered into a covenant, and made the most important decision two humans could ever make together. These friends made up our village.

I met my best man, Bobby, in Sunday school when we were five. Moments into class, he dared me to place a tack on another kid's seat. I took him up on it and got in big trouble. A friendship was birthed.

Next to him was Jaxon, another childhood friend who once visited me from Atlanta when I was in graduate school on the West Coast. I'm not sure if he was attracted by the weather, the ladies, or our friendship, but a few weeks later Jaxon packed up all his things, moved to California, and crashed on my sofa.

I met Howard and Dennis in college, where we enjoyed each other's company so much we petitioned to become roommates. I remember late-night battles on the SEGA Genesis, road trips up and down the East Coast, and deep fits of laughter whenever Dennis showed us his swollen testicle the size of a potato. (After months of urging, he finally went to the doctor and thankfully nothing was seriously wrong with him.) When I moved from Atlanta to Los Angeles, Howard hopped in the car to keep me company on those long stretches of I-20 in Texas where the exits seemed to be fifty miles apart.

I met my other groomsmen in Los Angeles. We were in a small group together, where we shared intimate secrets and leaned on each other for strength. Not every interaction was somber, though; there was plenty of laughter as well. Derrick, on a dare, once took off his prosthetic leg, jumped into the pool, and beat another friend in a race.

I smile when I see pictures of our wedding party, but it's not because of the outdated tuxedos and cummerbunds. What brings me joy are the many mountains and valleys we scaled together. But if I can be honest, the odometer on our friendship has long since stalled for all but two of my groomsmen. My relationship with one of my friends has changed so much I'm not even sure I'd want him to lower me to my final place of rest.

Neither time nor taste permits me to get into a detailed postmortem of what happened between my groomsmen and me. Suffice it to say there are various reasons for the demise of our friendships, with enough blame to go around. I screamed and cursed at Bobby one time because I thought he cheated on a few holes during a round of golf. Which was silly, because we both had picked up the game a few months before and had yet to break a hundred. It took me a few years to move past my hubris and say I was sorry. Bobby accepted. While we still talk from time to time, it hasn't been the same.

Another of my groomsmen got married and soon began abusing his wife. I helped her get to safety before confronting my friend. To this day he refuses to speak to me. I'm sad but comforted that I did what was right.

Derrick told me he's no longer a Christian. About a year or two later he divorced and moved to Africa.

As for three of the others, there's not much to tell. We live far apart and have sunken more and more into our own worlds. Over time the calls and interactions became less until they all but ceased, save for direct messages on social media once every eighteen months.

Then there's the one that most irritates me. I worked really hard to preserve my friendship with Howard. I'd call and we would have substantive conversations, after which I'd feel full as if I'd eaten just a bite too much of my favorite food. But then it hit me: we never played tennis. Not in the literal sense—rather, I was always the one calling, and Howard never returned my "serve" by calling me back. While I know I shouldn't play these games, I decided not to call to test my theory. Howard and I went a whole year without speaking until he called me moments after I'd opened Christmas gifts with the kids. We picked up right where we left off, but some months later I realized yet again we weren't playing tennis. Maybe I'm wrong, but I interpreted his lack of initiative as, "He's just not that into you."

In the years since our wedding, God has been kind and replaced those friendships with new ones, which have come at the most opportune moments. I don't know how I would have endured five tearful years at St. Jude Children's Hospital with my middle son if it weren't for new friends in Memphis, none of whom were around when Korie and I exchanged nuptials. But for the most part, these new relationships have also receded like the tide. I've come to the conclusion that friends are like people who join you with a cup of cold water during stretches of life's marathon. They are there for a few miles to refresh and strengthen you, then drift back into the crowd. Friends are more seasonal than permanent.

This is just one of many things I would share with my young self at the altar. The temporal nature of relationships is not a sign of failure but is instead the natural course of things. While I grieve the passing of my "I wills," I also give thanks for the stretch of road they ran with me. Their friendship was a real gift. To be clear, this book is not about the people who will come in and out of our lives but is more focused on what Gordon MacDonald refers to as our "happy few," the rare ones who will be there for the whole marathon.

THE PURSUIT OF FRIENDSHIP

My story isn't unique. Our deepest desire is to know and be known. We were made for relationships. In the creation account, God surveys his work and exhales in joyous satisfaction, "It's good." Only once does he pronounce, "Not good," and that's when Adam is alone. To remedy this, God creates Eve, pairs her with Adam, and instructs them to be in oneness with each other. God's command is far more than sexual. In fact, Adam and Eve's sexual union illustrates the comprehensive harmony of their souls. In the deepest sense, they are called into friendship.

To be human is to have an innate need to be in oneness with others. Let's look at this another way. Think of your most frustrating moments in life. More often than not, they are related to some relational breakdown. A dad who walked out on you. A mother who was impossible to please.

A person you trusted who took advantage of you. Someone you tried to play tennis with who never returned your serve. An individual you could have been friends with until they lied or gossiped about you. I could go on.

With enough of these slights over time, we lose our will to fight for friendship. We tell ourselves it's not worth the trouble and settle into the status quo of shallow interactions with others. But another part of us won't stop longing for the trouble. This yin and yang of the human condition is what it means to be created in the image of God. God the Father, Son, and Holy Spirit formed their own triad of "I will. I did"—this is what theologians call the Trinity. Life, therefore, is most frustrating when we live in isolation and most meaningful when we travel with our tribe of "I will. I did."

Read any study on human satisfaction and you will see the paramount role of relationships with others. And yet, so many of us readily exchange friendship and community for success and achievement, only to conclude there is no amount of success that can satiate our drive for fulfillment or happiness. I know firsthand. Like most, I spent my twenties and thirties on a sojourn up Mount Significance. By twenty-five I had accrued two degrees. In my thirties I began doctoral studies. Before forty I had written three books. In fact, when my first book was shipped to me weeks before its publication, I pulled my father's first book off my shelf to compare the publishing date so I could know how old he was when he wrote *his* first book. I sighed in relief over the revelation I was three years younger than Pops when my first offering was to be published. Yes, I was that driven (or sick). Later, I went on to pioneer a rare multiethnic megachurch with thousands in membership and launch an organization to help the multiethnic church become the new normal in America. The invitations to speak were so vast, it was all I could do to keep up as I flew well over a hundred thousand miles every year. But each time I scanned my ticket to board another flight and heard the gate agent congratulate me on my elite status with their airline, something felt amiss. I was successful and unhappy all at once. So as forty loomed, I knew I needed to make significant changes.

On my fortieth birthday, I sat out on a patio overlooking a golf course, refreshed by the cool breeze and determined to spend the second half of my life scaling a different mountain. I resolved to be more intentional and dedicated to cultivating friendships with those I deemed could be my "I will. I did." Sure, I had collected beyond my fair share of acquaintances and associates, but I was after more. So I began to think about what a friend should be. While a definition eluded me, a picture of what I was hungry for began to emerge. I was after a happy few who would make a shared treaty with me, and I with them.

It's been said home is the place where they have to let you in. While it's a reach to say I'm friends with each of my family members, our relationships thrive because we share a mutual, understood responsibility for one another. This is what the Greek philosopher Aristotle meant more than two thousand years ago when he described the "friendship ladder." Some friendships are based on utility and pleasure; they are transactional in nature and tend to be very thin and short-lived. Many successful people complain about loneliness and the fatigue of experiencing relationships gone south because others have cozied up to them based on what they bring to the table. Some women sigh at being esteemed solely for their looks. There are also men put off by some women's perceived "gold digging" motives, which reduce them to what they produce. These transactional relationships supersede romance.

At the highest levels of friendship—what we might call our "I will. I did"—Aristotle describes "perfect friendship" as a shared commitment to one another's well-being based on an ethic outside either party.[1] Aristotle is referencing a kind of friendship based on a mutual appreciation of values. Unlike utility friendships, which lack depth, this "perfect" friendship moves beyond a person's performance and instead values them for who they are. Utilitarian friendships are thin and temporal, while value-driven friendships are thick and enduring. I want to not only receive but also give this kind of friendship.

This "perfect friendship" is seen in many families. When my sibling had to do a hard reset on her life due to an unexpected betrayal and a nasty divorce, I was there to help. My family and I were not going to let her drop out of the marathon, nor were we going to just run a few miles. We were all in. When I have likewise found myself in a pinch, my family has stood by me, even when others took a few steps back. This is what family does. And in a way that goes beyond DNA, this is what friendship is.

Not too long ago, my Aunt Hattie died. Hattie was not my father's sister. In fact, we share no genetics. When my father's parents migrated from the South to New Jersey in the early part of the twentieth century, they found themselves disoriented as they settled into life in a foreign place, having just escaped the tyranny of Jim Crow. Soon after their arrival, Hattie and her husband embraced them and made sure they had all they needed as they sought to make a life of their own. Weekends they were over at each other's homes playing cards. Sundays they were shoulder to shoulder at church. They showed my grandparents the ropes and potential pitfalls in their new environment. When my father or his sisters acted up, Aunt Hattie was there with a word of correction. When my grandmother was tied up with another commitment while my grandfather was at work, Aunt Hattie was there. All along Aunt Hattie and her family sent the message to my grandparents, "You will make it. I am responsible for you." And when my Nana and Pop-pop died a half century later, Aunt Hattie was there as they were lowered into the grave. In her own way, she declared, "I will. I did."

In the Christian faith, Jesus calls his followers "friends" (John 15:15-17). This description came days before his crucifixion, when he committed the ultimate act of friendship. His disciples throughout history firmly believe that friendship with Jesus fights against the temporal nature of most relationships and spans beyond the grave into eternity. With his costly sacrifice, Jesus let it be known, "I will. I did."

COMMITTED TO FRIENDSHIP

Every other year I venture out to Santa Cruz, California, to speak at a conference. Not far from where we meet is a forest thick with redwood trees. Redwoods are known to grow to well over two hundred feet, even though their shallow roots run no deeper than five or six feet. These trees can live for hundreds of years, even over a thousand. Redwoods seem to defy the laws of physics given their height and shallow roots. But if you take a closer look, you'll see redwoods are not by themselves. Instead, they grow in thick groves with other redwoods, where their roots comingle with roots from other trees to form a network of friendship. They may start out as individuals, but over time they grow as one.[2] The key to their longevity is friendship.

Any social science study will tell you relationships are key to happiness and well-being. But there's more.

Friendship isn't just an elective in the course of life, it's required. In my line of work I've seen many successful leaders have a moral meltdown and implode. A cursory investigation more times than not reveals an isolated person who was incarcerated in solitary confinement by their own success. Solomon, the most successful king to have ever lived, put words to this when out of his vast wisdom he said,

> Two are better than one, because they have a good reward for their toil. For if they fall, one will lift up his fellow. But woe to him who is alone when he falls and has not another to lift him up! Again, if two lie together, they keep warm, but how can one keep warm alone? And though a man might prevail against one who is alone, two will withstand him—a threefold cord is not quickly broken. (Ecclesiastes 4:9-12)

We would do well to keep in mind that Solomon's words on the necessity of friendship were written toward the end of his life, well after he scaled his own Mount Significance. His accomplishments were unprecedented. Solomon constructed one of the seven wonders of the ancient world and accrued unbelievable amounts of money and women. He denied himself no pleasure. At the same time, he was deeply unfulfilled. A psychiatrist once quipped if she had to render a diagnosis on Solomon, she wouldn't hesitate to pronounce his depression. I can't help but wonder, *Where are Solomon's "I will. I dids"?* At some point, achievement surpassed friendship for him.

Solomon should have learned from his father, King David. Yes, David achieved a lot as he ushered Israel into her golden age. He rushed to battle, enlarged Israel's territory, and brought peace and economic stability to the nation. But David was also a man of great joy. Read his many psalms—he not only sings but also exhorts us to sing and clap and shout and dance. Yes, dance! His wife once looked at him with contempt as he danced in the streets with all his might. Sure, David had his down moments like all of us, but the image he portrays is hardly one of depression but its antithesis: joy.

We should not miss the link between David's joy and his warrior-like commitment to friendship, most notably with Jonathan. The two met after David's famous defeat of Goliath. There they pledged an oath to each other, where they said in their own words, "You will make it. I am responsible for you." Jonathan, the prince of Israel, sacrificed his own position and risked death when his father hurled a spear at him, all for his friendship with David. Over the course of their friendship, they appealed to an ethic outside of themselves as they were strengthened by each other in the Lord. And when Jonathan was slain, David composed a beautiful lament. Their masculine friendship plumbed such rare depths that some scholars throughout the years have even questioned their sexuality. By their example,

David and Jonathan reveal the line between sorrow and joy can be spelled with the word *friendship*.

Easier said than done. Our current cultural moment makes rich, life-giving friendships like the one David and Jonathan shared a challenge. We are connected like never before, yet isolated and lonely like never before. MIT professor Sherry Turkle sets forth this point in her book *Alone Together: Why We Expect More from Technology and Less From Each Other*. She puts words to what many of us feel:

> Technology is seductive when what it offers meets our human vulnerabilities. And as it turns out, we are very vulnerable indeed. We are lonely but fearful of intimacy. Digital connections . . . offer the illusion of companionship without the demands of friendship. Our networked life allows us to hide from each other, even as we are tethered to each other. We'd rather text than talk.[3]

Who cannot relate in the digital age to the irony of being overconnected and lonely all at once? Yet Chief Justice John Roberts, speaking at his son's middle school graduation, exhorted the young graduates to see the loneliness of our age as a pathway to friendship:

> From time to time in the years to come, I hope you will be treated unfairly, so that you will come to

know the value of justice. I hope that you will suffer
betrayal because that will teach you the importance
of loyalty. Sorry to say, but I hope you will be lonely
from time to time so that you don't take friends for
granted. . . . I hope you'll be ignored so you know the
importance of listening to others, and I hope you
will have just enough pain to learn compassion.
Whether I wish these things or not, they're going to
happen. And whether you benefit from them or not
will depend upon your ability to see the message in
your misfortunes.[4]

Don't get me wrong, I'm hardly advocating for an anti-
digital posture that involves getting rid of your smart-
phones and deleting all your social media apps. The
challenge with our cultural moment is the ease with which
we create communities where we can block, unfriend, or
mute anyone who doesn't agree with us. The result is a
utilitarian, thin community, and worse yet, a lack of resil-
iency toward the inevitable slights and idiosyncrasies that
occur along the journey of real, enduring friendship.

I was invited recently to speak to a very prominent
men's college basketball team. Before I spoke, the coach
allowed me to sit in on practice and take a tour of their
state-of-the-art facilities. As the tour was winding down,
we walked into the locker room, where I was struck by the
silence and the sight of every player scrolling on their

phones. My mind immediately drifted back to my mediocre high school athlete days when our locker rooms were filled with chatter and interactions with one another. We would laugh, strike each other with wet towels, and crack jokes. No such thing on this day. The juxtaposition could not have been more stark. Outside the locker room, I asked the coach if things were always so quiet. He nodded sadly and confessed that his greatest challenge was no longer finding talent but creating chemistry, a thick community where the players could translate their understanding of one another into cohesiveness out on the court.

You may not be part of a sports team, but you probably know the challenges of friendship. This is why we need coaching on how to give and receive friendship. The apostle Paul, one of the most successful leaders in world history, provides us with the essentials for substantive, enduring friendships. By examining Paul's wisdom in the book of Philemon, we can learn to have friendships that stand the tests of time. Let's look together to see how we can have friendships that go with us to our graves.

1

WHY FRIENDSHIPS ARE SO HARD

We would be hard-pressed to find a more misquoted statement in history than the one attributed to the writer G. K. Chesterton. In response to a newspaper's question, "What is the problem with the world?" he tersely quipped, "I am." While this story is factually untrue, the point is completely biblical. Human experience, world history, and theology supply ample evidence for this apocryphal tale. But what is even more uncomfortable and seldom discussed is the link between the self and society, as this story suggests that the problem of the individual never remains with the individual but has an uncanny habit of contaminating those around them.

Whatever word we choose for what ails humanity—sin, dysfunction, immorality, issues—we must investigate how it impacts those around us. Until we get a grasp on the contagion of sin, we have no hope of friendship that endures the arc of time.

Sin is the decision to act independently of God. Nothing more, nothing less. I'm not sure where you are as it stands regarding God or sin, but if a person does not believe in the two, they are sitting on the defense stand, not God.

In the Garden of Eden, God makes one prohibition: to refrain from eating of the tree of the knowledge of good and evil. Sometime later, Satan entices Eve to eat. She then turns to her husband, who eats as well. Their decision to act independently of God had profound relational and societal consequences. Previously described as being naked and unashamed, Adam and Eve were completely vulnerable, transparent, and authentic with each other. Sexual intercourse between a husband and wife is designed to be in the framework of a committed friendship where a treaty or covenant is made. Every time a husband and a wife engage in sexual intimacy, they are saying their own version of "I see the best and worst in you, and I accept you as is."

But notice Adam and Eve's first move after they sin: they find fig leaves and hide from each other. Intimacy, transparency, and authenticity are gone. What's more, they used to walk with God daily, experiencing a soul-level harmony that defies imagination. But when they decide to act independently of God, he has to come looking for them. And when they hear God walking, they hide. Their sin was not just personal. It tore at the fabric of their relationship with each other as husband and wife and their friendship with God.

Sin now becomes a part of humanity's genetic code. David acknowledges he was born in sin. Paul says sin entered the world through Adam and has infected everyone, even creation. And if anyone does not believe our natural disposition is one of inherited sin, they must not have children. Why is it children never need to take a class on how to lie or be selfish with their toys? Why, when I was once engaged in an important business dinner, did my young son—driven solely by his desire to be done with it all, with no thought for anyone but himself—demand at the top of his lungs it was time to go? Sin is just the way things are. We come into this world at a net negative.

Sin is also the problem with every relationship. Sin is why Adam and Eve's son, Cain, killed his brother, Abel. Sin is the reason Jacob and Esau were estranged for decades, as Jacob had swindled his own brother out of his birthright and was forced to flee his home. Sin ripped apart Joseph and his brothers. Sin is why Solomon viewed women as mere tools for his sexual satisfaction. Sin is why I cursed at my groomsman on the golf course, effectively ending the friendship. Sin is why my other groomsman was abusive to his wife, wrecking their intimacy and oneness. And sin is the reason for every divorce. Yes, we may call it adultery or irreconcilable differences, with the former a synonym for sin and the latter a fancy term for selfishness on the part of one or both parties. Why is friendship so hard? Because of sin's pervasive nature. Sin is never just about the individual; it is also deeply relational.

Renowned scientist Albert Einstein once wrote an ultimatum to his first wife, Mileva Maric. Ever the scientist, Einstein stated without a hint of kindness or compassion that she would make sure

> that my clothes and laundry are kept in good order; that I will receive my three meals regularly in my room; that my bedroom and study are kept neat, and especially that my desk is left for my use only. You will renounce all personal relations with me insofar as they are not completely necessary for social reasons. Specifically, you will forego my sitting at home with you; my going out or traveling with you. You will obey the following points in your relations with me: You will not expect any intimacy from me, nor will you reproach me in any way. You will stop talking to me if I request it. You will leave my bedroom or study immediately without protest if I request it.[1]

The relationship did not last. How could it when Einstein could not get outside of himself? Friendship will never endure when one party turns inward.

MEETING PHILEMON

There's a tiny book in the Bible the length of a short blog post. For years I saw no relevance in the book other than the way it irritated me as a black man. At the epicenter is a very understandable breach in the relationship between a slave owner named Philemon and his estranged "property," Onesimus. In the genesis of America, this book was used to perpetuate slavery and keep blacks in their place. If ever there was an appropriate use of the phrase "spiritual abuse," the way this text was wielded in the ante-bellum South is a perfect example. The great Howard Thurman, who was a mentor of sorts to Martin Luther King Jr., speaks of how his grandmother, a former slave, refused to read the book of Philemon because she found Paul way too complacent regarding the institution of slavery.

I share his grandmother's concern in wanting Paul to be far more vociferous in his denunciations of slavery. If I could, I'd scream at Paul to have him scream at Philemon, "We don't own people!" But Paul is loud in a different way. What he offers is the most potent vaccine to destroy the institution of slavery, something the people of South Africa have tried that we in America have not: friendship. Yes, the book of Philemon, this tiny blog post of a book, offers not only a visual of friendship but a roadmap of how we can experience friendship that will span the arc of time.

It's clear that this book is about friendship through Paul's appeal to Philemon: "For this perhaps is why he was parted from you for a while, that you might have him back forever, no longer as a bondservant but more than a bondservant, as a beloved brother—especially to me, but how much more to you, both in the flesh and in the Lord. So if you consider me your partner, *receive* him as you would *receive* me" (Philemon 15-17, emphasis mine). These words must have taken Philemon's breath away. In the original Greek, the word *receive* is a term of hospitality most often used when people ate together. In both Greek and Jewish culture of the time, people ate only with their social equals. This is why Jesus was always critiqued by the religious elite for eating with sinners and tax collectors. And now Paul is calling Philemon to transition from a utilitarian relationship of power to a brotherhood of friendship where he and Onesimus would be seated side by side as equals.

Before we write off Philemon as an enslaver of people, we would do well to pause and look for ourselves in this letter. Philemon's only interaction with Onesimus was from a top-down trajectory in which he wielded all the power. Onesimus simply had no recourse but to either do as instructed or take off. Their relationship is best defined by control, which continues to be a major subplot in human dynamics today, even in a post-slavery world.

There are plenty of Philemons today who would never remain in a relationship unless they held the keys. I once spent time with a very accomplished man named Chris who had built a successful business with hundreds of employees and was sought after by companies all over the world. He was also very lonely, a confession he made once over lunch. Chris couldn't understand this loneliness because, in his mind, he had friends. And in a way that made me squirm, he wanted to know why I had not reciprocated his overtures of friendship toward me.

I could have said something like, "Oh, Chris, you have friends. People love you. Stop being so hard on yourself." But I knew this was a lie. Instead, I gathered all my courage and said, "You're a very smart man, so I don't think what you will hear from me is new. We all have weaknesses, and yours is power. You use it to keep people in need of you. I've seen your gestures of friendship toward me, and I appreciate them. My struggle is that friendship is all about vulnerability, and it's impossible to be vulnerable with someone whose drug of choice is power, because they will leverage your weaknesses to their benefit while never sharing theirs." Sadly, Chris is still lonely because of his commitment to hold on to power at all costs.

This is exactly Philemon's problem. Onesimus, a common name that was given to slaves, means "useful." To Philemon, Paul says of Onesimus, "Formerly he was useless to you, but now he is indeed useful to you and to me" (Philemon 11). Paul gently calls out Philemon's utilitarian, power-centered disposition toward Onesimus. Theirs was not a friendship. Philemon was in control. He held all the cards, and as long as Onesimus produced, thereby proving his worth and usefulness, the relationship went well. But the moment Onesimus proved uncontrollable, he was deemed useless. This is why Roman law stipulated that a slave who ran away and was caught could be executed by crucifixion.

Look around and you will see a world dominated by Philemons—people who do not know how to travel the terrain of human relationships without being in control. One of the most difficult seasons of parenthood is when children become young adults. As a father of adult children, I can tell you the reason for the difficulty is we no longer have control, and if we try to clamp down and tighten the grip, we will have no relationship. My attempts at the role of Philemon have never ended well.

I could go on about shattered relationships due to an in-law's failed attempts at control because they did not approve of their child's choice of a partner. Or the overly sensitive spouse who, every time you broach a potentially combative subject, shuts down and weaponizes their tears. These are examples of veiled Philemons, who at their core cannot function without being in control.

You know you are in a relationship with a Philemon when they have a distorted view of loyalty. Should loyalty be a virtue in an authentic friendship? For sure. But the question is, loyalty to what? A real friend is loyal to their friend's well-being. This virtuous loyalty leads them to have hard conversations and tell them things they may not want to hear. This kind of loyalty refuses to lie to or for them. This is a good kind of loyalty—not the kind the power-hungry Philemons of the world want. They're after a narcissistic loyalty that has clearly defined boundaries. If you cross these boundaries you are canceled, and they will exercise their right to crucify the relationship.

One of the most painful moments in life is when you realize you're in a friendship with a Philemon. I was jarred by this revelation some time ago. Jason and I had a wonderful friendship where we talked almost every day. Our conversations ranged from sports to matters of the soul. When Jason asked me to help him, I did . . . most of the time. The first time I couldn't help him, he cut off communication for a month. When we finally talked, I called him out on his behavior. Jason agreed this was a problem for him. But sure enough, the same scenario played out a year later, and that time I refused to play along. I had come to see this very successful man was used to people orbiting around him. And when Jason didn't get his way, he removed them from his life.

There are two extremes when it comes to loneliness. On one side is Philemon, the person who has not fully grasped both the hurt they inflict on others and the reason why friendship is so elusive for them. On the other is Onesimus, the person who has absorbed the blunt force trauma of the hurt and knows for certain why friendship is so hard. The undercurrent to either extreme is sin.

MEETING ONESIMUS

While it's impossible to have true friendship with the Philemons of the world, it's just as arduous to venture into relationship with Onesimus. He has been hurt too much to lay himself bare in friendship.

I roll my eyes when scholars debate why Onesimus fled Philemon's home. The simple answer is Onesimus knew what all of us know: we were not created to be owned by another human. It is possible Philemon acted in some way to expedite Onesimus's plans, maybe through a harsh word or lashing out at him physically. But at some point Onesimus said his own version of "enough is enough" and took off unannounced. I imagine Philemon returning from some trip and calling for Onesimus with no response. Maybe Philemon asks his wife and son if they've seen Onesimus and they shake their heads. Days later it hits him—Onesimus is gone and never will return. Their distorted relationship is over.

We can take only so much until our hurt triggers the classic fight or flight mechanism. Onesimus chose flight. There are many people in our world who relate with Onesimus.

Much of pastoral ministry is focused on sorting out people's problems with others. Over time, I've heard the familiar refrain of people who no longer want to deal with drama. Women have sat in my office exhausted over some failed interaction with another woman, saying, "See, I just can't be friends with women; they're too much trouble." While I haven't heard a man articulate a similar kind of exhaustion, the fatigue is evident. My pastoral experiences bear witness with modern social science. In a recent survey from the Survey Center on American Life, less than half of men and four out of ten women reported being satisfied with their friendships.[2] The problem is relationships *are* drama, and I don't mean this in a negative way. Whose life is not made up of mountaintops and deep valleys? Add to this the sin we all bring into our relationships, and we have what every good movie or book has—conflict. If we are not up for the drama, we are not ready for friendship.

The woman who announces she is finished with female relationships speaks out of a well of hurt. Something has happened to her, and also to the man who never makes an effort to maintain friendships. Their inner Onesimus is speaking.

There are people on the dating scene who just can't seem to sustain a relationship because at some point they sabotage themselves and cut things off. There is hurt beneath the surface in many of these cases, likely attributed to some event where the person gave themselves in vulnerability only to have their heart broken. While they long for communion with others, their pain prevents them from getting too far. Over and over again, Onesimus lifts his head and points to the exit. If we are honest with ourselves, unresolved hurt wounds more of us than we'd like to admit.

Though we have been hurt, our response to the pain makes all the difference. Paul understood this, which is why he gives what many people of color perceive as the most awful instructions ever. Paul tells Onesimus he has to go back to Philemon (Philemon 12). Paul is after a new relationship between Philemon and Onesimus, one in which the old power dynamics are dismantled for equality to emerge. But Paul understands there is no possibility for this kind of brotherhood unless Onesimus takes the long road back to Colossae, faces the one who wronged him, and deals with the hurt.

We live in a culture where those who have been hurt are deified and the oppressor vilified. It goes without saying that we need to defend and advocate on behalf of those who have been abused, pushed to the margins, and wronged. However, we cannot become so fixated on Philemon that we neglect to focus on Onesimus. Yes, it's impossible to have a friendship with someone who hurts others, but it's also impossible to be friends with someone who has formed an identity around their hurt instead of dealing with it. The lead actor in the drama of our culture is no longer Philemon but Onesimus.

This is where Paul's letter to Philemon presents us with a challenge. Imagine taking this letter to various movie studios in the hopes it gets turned into a film. The problem that studio executives will have is there is no clear villain. Sure, Philemon is fraught with problems—he is a slaveowner, after all—but Onesimus doesn't have clean hands, either. Read just about any scholar, and they will tell you that when Onesimus decides to leave, he faces a dilemma any slave faces: How will he fund his flight? How will he eat? What will he do about travel and lodging expenses? It's a cold world out there, and Onesimus is ill suited to thrive in Roman society as a free person. So Onesimus does what most slaves would do—he steals from Philemon. Paul alludes to this when he says, "If he has wronged you at all, or owes you anything, charge that to my account" (Philemon 18). In the drama of their relationship, there is mutual culpability. Please don't hear this as "equal culpability," as if owning a person is on par with stealing possessions. Rather, "mutual culpability" is an admission that both have stolen from each other. Philemon has stolen Onesimus's freedom, and Onesimus has stolen Philemon's possessions.

This is what sin does and why friendship is so hard. Sin makes thieves of us all because the epicenter of sin is self. All of us are obsessed with our own gratification, and we will not stop until we are satisfied. Some men never make it to the marriage altar to know the joys of friendship with a wife because they are obsessed with taking from a woman's body to satisfy themselves. Others will never know the kind of friendship that covers the arc of "I will" to "I did" because they put others down to elevate themselves through gossip or slander. Some are like one man I know who always cozies up to the "cool kids." The moment he finds someone "cooler," he leaves to join the new group. This is a form of stealing by which people take from others' success to build their own image. And then there is the opposite dilemma, where people surround themselves with friends who share their same station in life, whether they have been hurt like them or are experiencing the same economic struggle. We understand friendship often begins on a note of affinity. The problem, however, is that when one friend begins to do better and emerges into a new stratum of well-being or success, the other person crucifies the friendship, no longer able to steal from their failure to feel good about themselves.

You may wonder if there is any hope for Philemon and Onesimus to be friends. How in the world will the two thieves sit at the table of friendship? This then leads us to ask questions of our own relationships. Is there any hope in a world marred by sin, which tears at the fabric of human relations, for deep, abiding friendship?

What follows are some of the most brilliant instructions on how Philemon and Onesimus can pivot from a master-slave relationship to one of brotherhood and friendship. Simply put, the letter to Philemon unlocks the door and shows the way to enduring friendship. If we heed Paul's instructions, we will know the joys of sustained friendship and experience a kind of meaning that no paycheck or position can ever satisfy.

2

CULTIVATING FRIENDSHIP

In the early days of our marriage, the most stressful day of the month was when Korie sat down to balance the checkbook. Back then we did not have convenient apps to do the work. Instead, it took significant time to make sure the checkbook and bank statement were in agreement. This job landed on Korie's desk because I have an incredible threshold for ambiguity. Not once in all my single adult years did I think to balance my checkbook. Why "waste" precious time when I had a general idea of where things were in my mind? As is the case in most marriages, God gave me a partner who balances me out. Believe me when I tell you, if we are off by a nickel, my wife will spend however long it takes to find that nickel. This process Korie embarked on each month is called reconciliation. Over the years, I have realized many people focus more on ensuring their financial documents are in agreement rather than their own relationships.

If there's one word that sums up the book of Philemon, it is the word *reconciliation*. To be sure, reconciliation is not forgiveness. A person can forgive someone without being reconciled, but it is impossible to reconcile without forgiving. In the Christian faith, there are no loopholes for forgiveness. In Matthew 18, Jesus talks of the primacy of forgiveness for his followers and cements his point by telling a parable. An individual who was forgiven ten thousand talents by the king, the equivalent of billions of dollars today, then demanded payment from someone who owed him the equivalent of a number one at a fast-food joint. When the king heard about this person's unforgiveness, he said his version of "Are you kidding me?" and threw him in jail until he paid the last penny—an impossible task, which meant he would die in jail. Jesus ends his tale by saying we will meet the same fate if we do not forgive people from our hearts. His point is scary: a Christian who does not forgive is a contradiction in terms.

To forgive is to send away the offense, to throw away the scorecard. Corrie ten Boom forgave the Nazi concentration camp guard who played a part in her sister's death. One octogenarian, after decades of pent-up bitterness toward a father who had wronged him and had long since died, wrote a letter in which he scrawled, "I forgive you," and left it on his father's grave. Jonathan Irons extended forgiveness to the prosecutor and officials who threw him in jail for twenty-three years while they knew he was innocent of the crimes he was pronounced guilty of.

As essential as forgiveness is, Paul has his sights set on a higher ethic. He's after reconciliation, which has to do with the restoration of relationships. Remember, Paul appeals to Philemon to take Onesimus back, no longer as a slave but as a brother. Reconciliation is not an adventure back to the way things were but a sojourn into the desired future. Had Paul merely appealed for a repairing of the relationship, he would have been content with Onesimus returning to his position as a slave and Philemon behind the wheel of the relationship once again. Paul wants friendship, the former slave and slave master, now seated around the table in brotherhood.

What sin is to the demise of a friendship, reconciliation is to its future renewal. Because sin continues to permeate all of humanity, there will always be the need for reconciliation. What sin distorts, reconciliation revitalizes. There is a seminal difference between forgiveness and reconciliation—while there is no loophole for forgiveness because it takes one, there is always a loophole for reconciliation because it demands two. Paul wrote to the Romans, "If possible, so far as it depends on you, live peaceably with all" (Romans 12:18). I love this verse because Paul acknowledges that even when you do your absolute best, there will be times reconciliation doesn't happen because the other person refuses to bring the same energy.

Maybe this is a breath of fresh air for you. There's a sibling, friend, or acquaintance you haven't talked to for a significant period of time, a breach brought on by some offense. You've called, invited them to coffee, and sent an apology text or email with little to no response. Or if there has been a response, it's been walls and pushback and resistance. At some point you must tell yourself you've done your best while still hoping they will roll up their sleeves and do the work alongside you to renew the relationship.

Paul understands reconciliation requires two, which is why he takes the time to address *both* Philemon and Onesimus. Clearly, the letter is directed to Philemon in the hopes he will take Onesimus back as a brother. But it's also clear that Paul has talked to Onesimus, directing him to go back to Colossae and make things right with Philemon. Paul understands if there is any hope for the two to eat at the table of friendship, there must be a dual commitment to do the work of reconciliation.

But what does this work entail? The letter of Philemon centers around three characters who each personify a foundational attribute of the work of reconciliation. Paul, who embodies truth, says some hard, truth-filled things to both Onesimus and Philemon. He tells Onesimus to go back, and he tells Philemon to welcome Onesimus no longer as a slave but now as a brother.

When a relationship flounders, there can be no hope for renewal without truth. We must do what football teams do after the big weekend game: replay the film and investigate the painful truth about what happened, good and bad, but ultimately for the better. This process of truth is hard for the offender because they do not want to be reminded of the hurt they inflicted. But if people are not willing to analyze what happened, they are not ready for reconciliation.

The one who has been hurt also needs to go through the journey of truth. Many people when they get hurt tend to flinch in denial as if they really weren't bothered or offended. Pushing down the hurt hinders any possibility of true friendship with the one who harmed us and others as well.

The great North African theologian Augustine defined friendship as "a complete harmony of minds and purpose."[1] Attaining this kind of harmony demands not only transparency but also truth. Augustine's two deepest friends were Alypius and Nebridius, rare gifts who functioned as his "I will. I did." Nebridius was a wealthy man, and his commitment to Augustine was so complete that he moved from his home in Carthage to follow Augustine to Milan. However, unlike the masses, Nebridius was not enamored with Augustine. Reflecting on their years of friendship, Augustine remembered Nebridius's rebukes.[2] What made Augustine a better man was the gift of truth from his friend.

Like all children, my kids had the propensity to lie from time to time. Having grown up in a home where the truth was demanded of me, I knew how uninspiring it could be to raise my voice and make threats until I got to the bottom of it all. Instead, I needed to dig beneath the surface with my children as to why they should be committed to speaking truth. It was around this time I heard a sermon that left a deep impression on me. For the life of me I can't remember what the subject was about, not because the speaker was boring but because the one thing he said so captivated my thinking everything else faded from memory. He said lying is listed among the abominable sins (Proverbs 12:22) because you cannot have relationship with a liar. God hates lying because he so deeply loves and values a friendship with us, and nothing impedes relationship like a lie. For the rest of their childhood, whenever I caught my children in a lie, I sat them down and said, "Daddy is hurt right now because I want so badly to have a relationship with you, but your choosing to not be truthful with me is getting in the way." There can be no relationship without truth.

It's one thing to speak the truth, but the great question remains: What will we on the receiving end of truth do with it once it is spoken? This is where repentance comes into play. Enduring friendship assumes sin. When we see the sin, we must speak the truth. And when confronted with the truth we must walk the road of repentance, which means turning in the opposite direction. Repentance is personified in the book of Philemon by Onesimus. Paul makes Onesimus go back to the scene of the crime because he understands that without repentance, or turning back, there can never be friendship.

The Greek word for *repentance* means a change of mind, which implies a change of direction. Repentance is different from confession because confession is a change in words, a verbal agreement with the one who was hurt that what you did was wrong. Repentance is a change in actions and behavior. If anyone is in relationship with someone who continues to cause harm and refuses to change their behavior, we call this abuse. And to be clear, please don't interpret reconciliation as making amends with an abuser in any form, whether verbal, emotional, spiritual, and so on. Let us remember that God is a God of both forgiveness and justice. If you have been assaulted or wronged in any legal sense, you need to take reconciliation off the table and even set this book down if you are in search of wisdom on how to interact with the person who puts their hands on you or refuses to change their harmful behavior toward you.

But no matter how much I acknowledge and turn from the harm I caused by my gossip, slander, lies, or other forms of betrayal, none of this works without grace, which is personified by Philemon. Paul can speak truth and Onesimus can make the almost one-hundred-mile trek back to

Colossae, but if Philemon does not put down his power and control, pick up grace, and extend it to Onesimus, their relationship and even Onesimus's life is over. And let's not forget the point of mutual culpability. Onesimus is not the only one in need of grace. So is Philemon, and it can be argued that the latter's need is even more severe.

When Korie and I knew our relationship was headed toward marriage, we thought it best to literally bring all our bills to the table. By far, this was the most vulnerable we had been with each other. We sat at my little kitchen table, which was scattered with credit card and student loan bills. Sure, there were questions and a few raised eyebrows, but when the conversation was over, we decided to continue the journey. This decision into enduring friendship was also based on another one: that we would assume each other's debts. In her own way, Korie said my debts would become hers. Once married, she would work to pay off not *my* debts but *ours*. Likewise, I said Korie's debts would become mine, which meant I would work to pay not *her* debts but *ours*. We call this grace, and our motivation for this is the cross, where Jesus assumed our debts that we might become friends with God.

Of course, friendship outside of the marriage covenant is not as demanding. However, having enduring friendships necessitates grace, whereupon entering the friendship we realize they come with debt, and so do we. At no point will either of us be morally free of sin. If this friendship is to make it, we must be committed to bearing one another's burdens (Galatians 6:2), which in context has to do with a person who has sinned. There is no lasting friendship without grace.

Truth, repentance, and grace are the triad of renewed and reconciled relationships. If you want to have sustained friendships over the course of your life, you must accept that you will at various points be Onesimus and Philemon—offender and offended. This is what sin does to us all. But where there is a commitment to truth, walking the road of repentance, and extending grace, the once tattered relationship can live into its desired future where a beautiful friendship emerges and extends over time.

PART ONE

TRUTH

3

HALOS AND HORNS

grew up in Atlanta in the 1980s, which meant field trips to Stone Mountain where the grand finale was a laser show and celebration of the leaders of the Confederacy. I could not have been past second or third grade, so my Civil War knowledge was likely deficient and without a doubt absent of any nuance. Be that what it may, I still felt an innate sense something was off. Around the same time, I became obsessed with the television show *The Dukes of Hazzard*, which featured the General Lee, an orange car with a Confederate flag painted on top. The sight of the car speeding through the rural roads of the South accompanied by the "Dixie" anthem never did sit right with me, but none of this compelled me to change the channel and say goodbye to my beloved Daisy Duke.

A few decades later I picked up a biography on Robert E. Lee. I didn't buy the book because I needed evidence he

was a bad guy; I was just curious as to how bad of a person
he was. When I finished, I wasn't quite sure what to think
of him. Lee was a thorough racist who believed in the
moral superiority of whites. At the same time, he had inherited some slaves and went about the task of emancipation. He was offered the opportunity to lead the Union
army and actually gave it some thought. In the end he
turned Lincoln down and led the Confederate army, but
not because of some deeply held convictions over their
cause. Rather, Lee was loyal to Virginia and felt obligated
to fight for her, and Virginia just happened to be on the
wrong side of the Mason-Dixon Line and history. I was
floored when I learned Lee considered slavery a moral and
political evil. By the time I closed the book I realized he
was not as bad as I thought he was, yet at the same time
he was no angel. Lee was a complicated person.

I then thought about people in the Bible, people like
David, who was an adulterer and murderer, yet God called
him a man after his own heart. Solomon is known as the
wisest person who ever lived, but at the same time he was
insanely foolish and cruel with women. One of my favorite
authors is Brennan Manning, who has a unique ability to
speak to the deepest places of our souls. If you decide to
read him, keep in mind he was also an alcoholic, a struggle
he nursed all the way to his grave.

The same is true for Philemon and Onesimus. Not long
after Onesimus steals from Philemon and makes his way

to Paul, Paul refers to him as "my child" and says he is sending Onesimus, "my very heart," back to Philemon (Philemon 10, 12). This is peculiar language to describe a thief, especially used by someone who is not related by blood in reference to another. Paul begins with a commendation of Philemon when he says he thanks God always for him (Philemon 4). He then goes on to say he thinks of Philemon's love and faith, and how he has personally derived joy and comfort from Philemon who has refreshed the hearts of the saints (Philemon 7). If Paul were to post these terms of endearment about an enslaver today, he would be publicly flogged in the social media town square by a society that leaves less and less room for the complicated.

And then there's you and me and the people around us. If we are honest with ourselves, we have to conclude horns don't fit us perfectly, and neither do halos. We are not as bad as we think we are, nor are we as good. Neither is the one who wronged us. We are all incredibly complicated people.

We would do well to be mindful of this when we venture down the path of friendship. There is no hurt like that which comes from someone you've opened your heart to. When the betrayal happens, we remove the halo we placed on them and replace it with horns, viewing them solely through the lens of the wrong they inflicted on us. The husband whose wife cheated could not make the relationship work because he could not see past her infidelity. Your bestie you did the annual girl's trip with gossiped about you and caused the death of your friendship, and now you see only her betrayal.

Psychiatrists have coined the term *fundamental attribution error*. When you make a mistake I blame it on your character, but when I make the same error, I ascribe it to circumstances. For example, if I'm late to work, it's because my alarm didn't go off and there was an unusual amount of traffic on the freeway. But when you are late to work, it's because you're lazy and lack a sufficient work ethic. Fundamental attribution error says we are gracious with ourselves because we believe we are good people and brutal with others because they're not as good as us. We take photos of people on their worst days and remember them that way forever while we photoshop ourselves, convinced we are better than others, especially the ones who hurt us.

When we fail to allow for nuance and complication, we set the table for short-lived friendships that never resurrect from the graveyard of offense and betrayal. Our society is rife with the hypocrisy of cancel culture. If we want to close the door on any possibility of long-term friendship, we will be promiscuous with grace in regard to ourselves and celibate with the same grace when it comes to others. We will leave margin for nuance in our own life while we allow none for the person across the table from us. Nothing will end a relationship faster than this.

Reconciliation is possible for Philemon and Onesimus because Paul allows for the scandalous truth of nuance and complexity. He refuses to cast Philemon aside because he owns a slave, and he will not allow Philemon to cancel Onesimus because he has stolen from him. The truth is that the same one who owns people loves Jesus and has shared his love with many others. And the very one who is a thief Paul claims as his child and heart.

This truth undoes us when we realize God doesn't love Philemon more than he does Onesimus. The blood of Jesus is for the betrayed and the betrayer, the oppressed and the oppressor, the lynched and the lynch mob, the faithful and the adulterer. God does not view us through our worst moments, and for this I'm thankful. Until we arrive at this truth, which is sure to undo us, we will never be ready for the long road of enduring friendship.

4

RISKY TRUTH

Facing Up to the Beast

When the dust settled from the long-awaited decimation of apartheid, the new Republic of South Africa hungered for more. Dissatisfied with the legal victory, they moved to the work of reconciliation through the Truth and Reconciliation Commission. At its core, the commission was a series of gatherings whereby those who had committed crimes against humanity could confess the truth of their atrocities to those they had violated in the hopes of forgiveness and a renewed community. As you can well imagine, some pushed back and questioned the need to rehash what had occurred. *Must we go back to yesteryear to dig up the hurt?* they wondered.

In his book *No Future Without Forgiveness*, Bishop Desmond Tutu gives his response to those who wanted to circumvent the commissions: "Our common experience in fact is the opposite—that the past, far from disappearing or lying down and being quiet, has an embarrassing and persistent way of returning and haunting us unless it has been dealt with adequately. Unless we look the beast in the eye we find it has an uncanny habit of returning to hold us hostage."[1] Tutu argues the work of reconciliation necessitates a deep dive into the truth to examine the intricacies of the pain. Without this commitment to look the "beast" squarely in the eyes, there can be no movement forward on the path of friendship.

The journey of friendship is fraught with unavoidable hurt because those involved are marred by sin, or what some theologians call total depravity. Because of Adam and Eve's sin in the Garden, everyone who has since arrived on the scene of humanity has been colored by their transgression. Total depravity does not mean we are as sinful as we could be; it is not a statement of the depths of sin but more so the *extent* of sin. As one pastor says, "If sin were blue, we'd all be Smurfs." We are that completely colored by it. And since sin is not just individual but is a load-bearing kind of weight that bears down on human relations, causing relational fractures over the course of time, we are left with no recourse but to look the beast of sin in the eye if we are to move forward in reconciliation. If I could fiddle with Bishop Tutu's book title, we might very well call it *No Reconciliation Without Truth*.

While Paul references the truth of what caused the breach between Philemon and Onesimus, he does so in broad terms. He wishes for the two to sit down together and review what happened in the past if they are to sit at the table of friendship in the future. They must have a truth encounter. There is no other way around things.

The same holds true for you and me. As uncomfortable as it may seem, the adult child must talk to his father as to why he abandoned the family and failed to be present in his life. If estranged friends are to venture into their desired future, they must talk about why one person chose to betray the other's confidence. And if the business partnership between two best friends falls apart when one friend reneges on their oath, they must have a discussion about the breach of integrity.

There is a popular yet very unfortunate scene that plays out daily in the theater of human relations. A person will receive some unfortunate news from a third party about a friend of theirs, something along the lines of, "I hate to tell you this, but your friend just said this about you, or did xyz. Please don't say anything. I just thought you should know." I've been placed in this awkward situation more times than I care to count. It's awkward because I have to choose either confidentiality or betrayal of trust, which means choosing between the source of the information or my friend. Over the years I have sacrificed too many friendships on the altar of confidentiality, and I am not alone. In my younger days I bought into the myth that keeping things buttoned up would protect the conveyor of information and preserve the friendship at the same time. Instead, I found myself drifting away from the person I had built so much relational equity with, filled with increasing resentment as I wondered, *How could you?* With nowhere to go, the friendship ultimately floundered.

But we do have somewhere to go, and it's a place called truth. At some point I decided to run a cost-benefit analysis. On the one hand I could protect the messenger, who in just about every case was not on par relationally with the person they said had offended me, or I could seek to protect and strengthen the friendship while sacrificing the one who shared the information. Seen in this light, why in the world had I left so many friendships vulnerable just to keep a secret from someone who was barely an acquaintance?

It's dangerous to confront a friend. They may throw their hands in the air and end things altogether. They may not respond well. If a person has no willingness to deal with the truth, they are not ready for reconciliation. But the business of truth is a risky one. It's risky for the one who has been hurt because they have to muster up the faith and vulnerability to admit they were indeed hurt. And it is risky for the one who inflicted the wound because they must have the humility to be reminded of the error of their ways and the depth of their sins. Both share the joint risk that the trip back to what transpired may end the relationship.

But isn't this what a commitment to the truth does? It indeed will end the relationship as it was once known. There are only two possibilities when friends allow themselves to explore what happened. One is the termination of friendship forever. When we answer honestly and vulnerably to the hurt we caused, the other person could very well pack their bags and head for the exit. On the other hand, after we look the beast in the eye and extend grace and forgiveness, what emerges is not the old relationship but a new one, so markedly transformed it is like comparing a caterpillar to a butterfly. When we do not tell the truth, we risk—no, we guarantee—the death of the friendship. Run your own cost-benefit analysis, and you'll see that the best course of action is to stand squarely in front of the mirror and face the beast.

There is always the potential for liability when it comes to truth. Paul understands this. He knows the risk when he tells Onesimus he has to go back to Philemon. First there is the personal risk to Onesimus's life. Remember that Roman law stipulated Philemon was well within his rights to kill his once fugitive slave by crucifixion. We lose so much of the emotional context when we just read words on the page. I see Onesimus convening with an incarcerated Paul over a series of discipleship encounters.

Having led Onesimus to Christ and hearing his story and his crime, Paul agonizes over how to tell Onesimus that while he is glad to have him as a child in the faith, he has to go back and make amends with the one he stole from. The source of Paul's agony is his knowledge that Onesimus could refuse his counsel and cut off the newly minted friendship. To tell Onesimus the truth could mean the end of their relationship.

Paul runs the same risk with Philemon. In ways that defied the cultural norms of their time, Paul appeals to Philemon to take Onesimus back, no longer as a slave but as a brother. Maybe before he writes these truth-laden words, he pauses for a few minutes, hours, days even. Paul knows what is at stake. Philemon could head for the exit after reading his spiritual father's words and cut the relationship off. His commitment to kill Onesimus could also add to the death of his and Paul's friendship. The book of Philemon can be summed up by the word *reconciliation*, but it can also be summed up by the word *risk*. To tell the truth is to put relationships on the line.

We've all heard the phrase "the emperor has no clothes" from the ancient fable about an emperor who was a bit of a clothes horse, always wearing the latest fashion. One day, he hears of two clothes makers who weave the finest outfits. He places an order, but he doesn't know these two men are scam artists who don't make a thing. To perpetuate their ruse, they say the only people who can see the clothes they make are fit for office. Those who can't see their handiwork must then be unfit for their positions. Anxious to get an update on the outfit, the emperor sends two of his associates. When they look at the garments they don't see anything, but they remember that if they admit this, they are saying they are not qualified to hold their positions. So they lie to the emperor and say the clothes look exquisite. Finally, the day comes to wear the outfit. Though the emperor doesn't see the garments, he confesses his amazement at the clothes makers' work and "puts the clothes on." What follows is a grand parade with the emperor as the centerpiece of attention. All eyes are on the naked emperor, and no one has the courage to tell him the truth except for a child who shouts out what everyone sees—the king's nakedness.

Why did the emperor go through such embarrassment? Because no one was willing to tell him the truth. They were too interested in holding on to their own jobs and lives. This continues today. I think of how many people could have been saved the embarrassment of bankruptcy, divorce, or scandal if someone had told them the truth. These kinds of events do not happen all of a sudden but are the culmination of a long process filled with incremental compromises that people around them see, yet no one is willing to speak the truth.

Years ago when Korie and I were dating, we were part of a young adults group at our church. We spent a lot of time with other couples, most of whom got married and invited us to stand with them at the altar as part of their squadron of "I wills." Today, only Korie and I, along with one other couple out of ten, remain married. I am not surprised by the dissolution of their marriages, though I am deeply saddened. If I'm honest with you, I saw it coming long before they signed the papers, but I did not take the risk to say anything. Our friend Aaron got divorced in part because he was condescending and mean to his wife, Candace. Every time we went out, Aaron was correcting her and talking down to her. It got to the point where Korie needled me to say something. I did not. Worn down by him emotionally over the years, Candace finally had enough. While there are other reasons for the end of their marriage, his perceived superiority was a major factor.

I have a friend named Harold, though I'm not sure the word *friend* is accurate because it's impossible to get close to him. Harold grew up in an abusive home where he watched his father beat his mother. The message Harold left home with was to avoid conflict at all cost. Any sign of trouble and Harold would simply shut down and refuse to deal with issues. Don't get me wrong—Harold is an incredibly nice guy. The problem is that instead of looking the beast in the eye, he has a collection of very shallow relationships along with several divorces. I know it sounds weird to say a nice person has been divorced several times, but it makes sense when you realize the impossibility of having intimacy with a person who avoids conflict.

I feel bad about what happened to Aaron and Candace. And I've got to take some ownership over the sustained shallowness of my "friendship" with Harold. No, this isn't me taking ownership of things I shouldn't, and yes, I understand I can't make anyone do anything. The trouble is I never said anything, and the reasons for this are many: I was mired in my own career advancement. I was bogged down by my own problems and pressures. I didn't want to rock the boat or push people away. In the final analysis, I just didn't want to take the risk and force them to look the beast in the eye by telling them the truth.

In our friendship, Korie and I have discovered over the years that we each harbor trigger points—areas of our lives where if we venture past the line, we are guaranteed to provoke some undesired emotional response. We made this discovery in the early years of our friendship, and as is the case in many marriages, we poked and prodded in an effort to squeeze the person into our own image. Yet, when we fail to provoke the change we are hoping for and instead experience the opposite, we learn to stay away from the yellow tape where the chalk line of hurt lies. As a result, our relationships stagnate. The person who has been hurt hijacks the friendship through their sensitivity, while the other is equally complicit because they shut down, not wanting to be bothered by the trouble they know will follow if they raise the issue. Neither is willing to take the risk of facing the truth.

There's another ancient story, quite the opposite of the one involving the emperor with no clothes, but there are some similarities. Like the emperor who walked naked in the parade, this king experiences embarrassment as well. He has committed adultery, and in an effort to conceal his indiscretion, he commits murder. Thinking all is well, he is confronted by a man named Nathan, who decides to tell him the truth of his immorality. Think of the risk involved for Nathan. He could have been killed for his refusal to back away from the truth. What's more, he is a busy prophet and could have made an excuse to abrogate the messy business of being a truth teller—but he doesn't. In the end King David faces the truth, and he becomes known as a man after God's own heart.

Juxtapose this situation with that of Samson, a leader who lived a few generations before David. Like David, Samson has a weakness for women. And like David, Samson's weakness gets the best of him. But unlike David, Samson dies in bondage with no real lasting legacy. What's the difference? Why does one come out of his failure and the other is drowned by his? There is no Nathan who comes to Samson. No one speaks the truth to him. Seen in this light, are we not compelled to believe the power of truth in not only saving people from embarrassment but also in rerouting them to their God-ordained destiny in life?

Truth is a two-way street where we share the truth and position ourselves to receive truth all at once. I've been reminded of this many times over the years. Once, my friend Brent and I were sitting out on his back porch well into the night. As the hours wore on we moved closer to matters of the heart. Brent is an alcoholic who has given me permission to prod him any time to see how he is doing. I've also granted him backstage access to the secret places of my life.

"I think you care too much about what others think of you," Brent blurted out. After shifting in my seat, I wondered aloud why he would say such a thing. "It seems as if the larger your church has grown, the more attention you pay to your appearance," he said.

I reminded Brent there was an obvious answer to this: when you begin with twenty-six people in a living room, there aren't many financial options when it's time to buy a new pair of shoes, compared to the well over a thousand people who were coming to the church at this particular time.

"No, it's more than that," Brent pressed. "You seem to have a growing obsession with the exterior, and I'm worried you'll get to the point where reputation matters more than character." Ouch.

Friends tell the truth because they are more committed to your well-being and purpose in life than they are to being liked. When they weigh the pros and cons of this whole business of truth telling, they are willing to double down on truth even if it costs them the relationship. Without truth there can never be a friendship of substance, and over time the friendship will fade to the stands in the marathon of life.

5

THE PROBLEM
WITH WINNING

In her memoir *The Liars' Club,* Mary Karr tells of a time when her aunt and uncle got into an argument and neither side was willing to give in. Unable to resolve the issue, the husband took out a lumber saw and cut the house in half, and he and his wife lived on opposite sides for the next forty years. It's hard to believe this is a true story, especially because a sugar package precipitated their fight.

The graveyard of friendships is not always brought on by some cataclysmic event like an affair or a betrayal. Rather, the demise of many relationships is over life's "sugar packages"—those seemingly small things that have their way of derailing us.

Sometimes, what feels like a sugar package to one person is more like an earthquake to another. Confession: I'm horrible with names, and this has gotten me in trouble over the years. After service, Korie would often come down to the altar while I talked with people. There have been times when I was engaged in conversation with someone and didn't introduce them to my wife standing beside me. I readily confess I should have, but in most cases I didn't introduce them to Korie because I had forgotten their name. As a pastor who should know everyone's name in the congregation, saying, "Tell me your name again," would mean I'm a horrible pastor, right? Besides, making introductions just didn't seem like that big of a deal to me. In our attempts to get at the truth, Korie had to accept my reasons and realize I wasn't trying to leave her out. On the other hand, I had to acknowledge that what feels small to me isn't necessarily small. Left unresolved, however, these sugar packages could have become a wedge in our friendship, sending us emotionally to either side of our home.

You may have your own recollections of estranged friendships. Your friend didn't acknowledge you publicly. You were not invited to the event at their home. There was a spat over a card game. That quirky habit or eccentricity drove you nuts. They didn't respond to your call or text when you thought they should have. They still owe you the money you let them borrow even though you told yourself it was a gift before you lent it, and what you gave them only amounted to the price of a sugar package compared to the value of the relationship.

"Be slow to make friends, and even slower to walk away from them," I was once told. Sound advice I didn't always follow in my sprint up Mount Significance. I had no concept of losing, so when people did or said things that made me feel like a failure, I bludgeoned them with the truth, showing them how wrong they were and how right I was. My obsession with success wreaked chaos on my friendships because I was always bent on winning. This led me to steward truth in such a way that my objective became winning the argument rather than preserving the relationship.

When Paul writes Philemon, we should keep in mind that Paul is an apostle, part of a small fraternity of leaders who was selected by Christ to give oversight to the church. Paul is a pretty big deal, and Philemon knows it. How could he not when the church that meets in his home was started under the oversight and direction of Paul? When Paul places himself in the role of mediator between Philemon and Onesimus, he does so endowed with a lot of power. Paul could very well have made the book of Philemon even shorter by saying his version of "Take Onesimus back as a brother, because I said so." And that would be that.

But this is not Paul's way. In a move worthy of mimicry, Paul says, "Accordingly, though I am bold enough in Christ to command you to do what is required, yet for *love's sake I prefer to appeal to you*—I, Paul, an old man and now a prisoner also for Christ Jesus—*I appeal to you* for my child, Onesimus, whose father I became in my imprisonment" (Philemon 8-9, emphasis mine).

Paul doesn't throw his weight around or slam his apostolic authority on the table. Yes, he wants Philemon to heed his appeal, but this is secondary to his ultimate aspiration: the bonding of a friendship around the table of brotherhood. So what if Paul wins the argument? It means nothing if he loses the relationship.

Don't I know it. When our family looked for homes in the San Francisco Bay Area, we found one we really loved . . . or rather, one we could afford. The problem was it did not have central air. The real estate agent told us air conditioning wasn't a big deal since this part of the country was known for its pristine weather. I even called some people I knew who lived in the area and was told the same thing—outside of a few days of the year we wouldn't miss central air. It made sense to me, and given the craziness of the housing market, I felt we needed to make a move quickly. Korie felt otherwise. She did not think it wise to invest in a home that did not have central air. A back and forth ensued where I came at her with my best arguments. I reminded her of how much it would cost us to install central air. I regurgitated what my colleagues who lived in the area had already said. Korie retreated into silence, remaining unmoved in her position that this was not the best decision. I moved forward on the closing of the home with her silent resistance, content I had won the argument.

A few months after we moved, the Bay Area experienced the hottest summer on record. I am so not kidding. Of course, this *would* be the year San Francisco clocked in at over one hundred degrees for only the tenth time in its history. Korie and I didn't continue our argument; she simply slept on the floor because that was the only place she could get cool. Speaking of "cool," that was a good word to describe our friendship at the time. Not only had our relationship been thrown off track by our own sugar package called central air, but I had to come to terms with the fact that while I had won the argument, I had lost the relationship. It's a truth I keep bumping into over the decades of our friendship: when I win, we lose.

Telling the truth is essential in human relations, but unless truth is handled carefully as a scalpel to bring healing to a relationship, it can turn out to be more of a knife, which can kill. Truth is just that—a very sharp object that must be handled with great care. This is why we need to be careful with verses in the Bible that instruct us to "speak the truth in love" (Ephesians 4:15). Oftentimes, when we come into a situation where a wedge has driven people apart, we only have an idea of what happened—meaning we have perspective but not truth. Humility says we should come in seeking truth and not just declaring truth. Seeking truth changes our entire approach.

We get a glimpse of this in how Paul communicates with Philemon. The letter has a warm, familial tone. Again, he refers to Philemon as his brother multiple times and Onesimus as his son. Paul is self-deprecating, referring to himself as an old man. The letter to Philemon is a masterclass in how to wield truth, because the first thing Paul models to us is *how* we say something is just as important as *what* we say.

This is really key if we want to win the person more than the argument. We have to be careful with our words. Over the course of our marriage, Korie and I have learned in the heat of battle to say, "Give me a moment, I'm getting my words together." This is a great practice because there is incredible power in what we say, and once the words leave our mouths it's impossible to retrieve them.

There's another ancient parable about a man who slandered someone in his village. Word of the man's slander began to spread through the small village so that no one wanted anything to do with him. Stung by the ostracism, he paid a visit to the village priest, confessed his offense, and asked how he could remedy the situation. The village priest responded, "Oh, that's easy. Get a bag full of chicken feathers and place one feather on the doorstep of each home in the village where you slandered this man."

"That's it?" the man asked. The priest nodded and told him to come back after he placed the feathers. So the man set out and did exactly as he was told.

The next day he exclaimed with great satisfaction how he had followed through on the priest's advice. "One more thing," the priest said. "Go back and collect each of the feathers and place them back in the bag." Stunned, the man said, "There's no way I can do that. It's been windy, and who knows where those feathers are. I'll never be able to get them back." After a pause, the priest said, "And so it is with words. Once they leave your mouth you can never get them back." The man turned away, dejected.

How we say something is as important as what we say. Part of the reason why Paul is able to craft his words carefully is that he uses a medium called letter writing. It probably took him days to gather his words and write them down. Maybe he crafted several drafts, removed words, and inserted others. In our digital age where we can send the email, tweet, post, or direct message with a second's notice, we would do well to take a moment and get our words together.

Paul also stewards truth well because he affirms the good before he deals with the difficult. You don't need to spend a day studying Greek to know that verses four through seven come before verse eight in the book of Philemon. Paul begins by affirming some admirable things about Philemon—his faith and love, and how he has refreshed the hearts of all the saints. This is hardly flattery, which would be sin. Paul is being genuine. I can imagine Philemon unfolding the scroll and taking in Paul's words.

It's not every day one gets correspondence from an apostle of the church! Maybe his heart is beating fast. But to read about how this big-time apostle thinks so highly of him would surely lower his heart rate and make him more receptive to the truth.

We would do well to follow Paul's example. Instead of going straight for the jugular, let's pause and give pointed encouragement on the positive things we see in the person seated across from us. Again, I'm not suggesting flattery. Gossip is saying something behind a person's back we would never say to a person's face. Flattery is saying something to a person's face we would never say behind their back. If you would not say it to anyone else about them, then don't say it *to* them. But because we are all complicated people with good and bad traits, let's put in the time and effort to speak words of life to a person before we get to the business at hand. In fact, if I read Paul right, affirming the good is very much a part of the business at hand.

After Paul speaks some very hard truth, he says to Philemon, "At the same time, prepare a guest room for me, for I am hoping that through your prayers I will be graciously given to you" (Philemon 22). I always chuckle when I read this verse because Paul seems to be saying, "Let me stay in your home because I want to make sure you did what I asked you to do by taking Onesimus back." However, we know Paul does not intend to be passive aggressive in the least. Quite the opposite. His request to stay at Philemon's home is his way of saying, "I want the relationship." To Paul, connection has always been greater than correction. In fact, where there is no connection, there will be little likelihood of someone receiving the correction.

When you've been wronged by another and muster up the courage to sit down and have the conversation, what do you really want? If it's all about winning or proving a point, then truth will become a weapon, a knife, and you will win and lose at the same time. But if what you really seek is to win not the argument but the relationship, then truth will be handled with care, like a scalpel, and you'll be better positioned to win the person.

PART

TWO

REPENTANCE

6

THE LONG WALK
BACK TO COLOSSAE

What you do with the truth is one of the key questions of friendship. The relationship hangs in the balance in this tiny window of time between hearing the truth and responding to the truth. Paul may be a big-shot apostle, but I imagine it wasn't effortless for him to tell Onesimus he needed to go back to Colossae to tidy things up with Philemon. He probably gave it some thought and a lot of prayer because he knew the risk involved. Then the ball was in Onesimus's court: he would either receive the truth and make the long walk back to Colossae or he would dig in, firm in his justifications that he indeed is right while Philemon is wrong. By the time we finish the letter, we don't know what Onesimus decided. It is one of the Bible's greatest unsolved mysteries, and I think this is the point. The book of Philemon brings us to a fork in the road. Will we remain in Rome and never deal with the truth, or will we make the long walk back to Colossae and look the beast in the eye?

Onesimus's dilemma is played out every day in our world for the fortunate ones with people in their lives who love them enough to tell them hard things. Unfortunately, many if not most people respond by digging in and resisting the truth, with catastrophic results.

In 1986, two ships collided just off the coast of Russia in the Black Sea. An investigation ensued to get to the source of the collision. The conclusion was heart-breaking. This maritime calamity was not the result of mechanical failure, technological breakdown, or human error—just the opposite. Both ships saw each other coming. Both ships spoke truth, demanding the other move. Neither ship responded by changing course but instead chose to dig in, firm in their position. The result of their refusal to adjust to the truth was the loss of hundreds of lives.

We live in a society rife with individualism, and one of its hallmarks is an allergic reaction to any kind of correction, no matter how clearly the person is in the wrong. During the preflight announcements on a plane when the crew says it's time to switch phones to airplane mode, someone will usually still linger on their phone in conversation. The flight attendant may give them the side eye as if to say, "I don't want to embarrass you, but you just heard the announcement, so please get off your phone."

If they refuse to respond to the message, the flight attendant has no recourse but to go over and reiterate the message they just heard. I have witnessed clearly annoyed passengers who either huff and puff while reluctantly getting off the phone or who choose to ignore the message altogether. Neither is an appropriate response to the correction they have just received. As my mother used to drill into my and my siblings' heads when we were coming up, "Obedience is doing what you're told, when you're told, with a happy heart." If this is the case, my flight-mates were far from obedient.

I sometimes think that people who violate such clear rules must be lonely people. If they will not put their laptop away as we are leaving the gate for the runway when they have just been told to do so, there is not much hope they will receive truth from those who really love them over the morsel of gossip they shared, the lie they told, or the breach of integrity they committed.

The Bible has a harsh word for people who reject the truth, determined to do life on their own terms—a *fool*. This is God's language, not mine. This word is used most often in the book of Proverbs, which is in the section called Wisdom literature. Proverbs is encapsulated in one word: *listen*. Wisdom in Proverbs is personified as a woman who cries aloud in the streets to those who pass by. We may say Lady Wisdom speaks the truth. A wise person listens and responds to the truth by making whatever adjustments are appropriate. Conversely, a fool is not necessarily an ignorant person who does not know any better, but rather, someone who hears the truth and stays entrenched in their belief that they are right while Lady Wisdom is wrong. The book of Proverbs for all its wisdom is a very simple book with a clear message. To discern if the person you are doing life with is wise or foolish, see how they respond to truth. Fools refuse to move. Wise people change. It's impossible to have a friendship with a fool.

The message of Proverbs in which Lady Wisdom pleads with people to listen leaves us with a more accessible standard for wisdom. We often envision the wise person as a weathered sage seated in a rocking chair, holding court before a crowd of much younger people. However, the Bible does not limit wisdom to a certain age; instead, wisdom is seen primarily in how a person responds to the truth. I'm encouraged by this, because a three-year-old can be wise while a ninety-three-year-old can be foolish.

The question before Onesimus is whether he will choose the path of wisdom or the path of fools. If he chooses to go anywhere else but Colossae, he is a fool. But if he does a U-turn and makes the almost one-hundred-mile trek back to Philemon's house in response to the truth he has heard from Paul, he is wise. Wisdom is synonymous with repentance, and to repent is to change.

Repentance is not confession. To confess is to change your words, but to repent is to change your actions.

Repentance is the admission you were headed in the wrong direction. You must stop and do a one-hundred-and-eighty-degree turn in the opposite direction. For Onesimus, repentance is the acknowledgment he cannot stay in Rome. He has to go in the opposite direction back to Colossae to make things right.

Repentance, this turning away from where you are in an effort to change, is not a one-time act but a present day-to-day walk. It's theologically incorrect to say we *have* repented, as if the issue will never resurface or we will never fail again. A more theologically and grammatically correct way to say it is we *are* repenting. Every day the alcoholic chooses to refrain from the martini is a day of repentance. Every moment the former adulterer resists the temptation to engage in some emotional or physical tryst is a few more steps on the road of repentance. And every time we choose to be people of integrity who "swear to their own hurt" (Psalm 15:4), we walk another mile on our way back to Colossae. Change is not a destination but a journey where we wake up one day surprised by how far we are from Rome, the place we began.

For several years, Jason and I nurtured a friendship that led us to decide to work together because we knew each other so well. But things soon became complicated between us. I began to notice some troubling patterns in his work habits, and when I challenged him on these things, he responded by going around to various staff and raising questions about me. The revelation of his actions so startled me that I literally felt winded. I could almost feel the waters of unforgiveness rising in my heart. Over time, I was faced not only with the truth of his sin but also my own sin in my refusal to forgive. My decision to hold on to the offense soon began to color my actions with others. I became more reserved. Transparency and vulnerability, two traits I once prided myself on, were nowhere to be found. I was frustrated I had given him a power over me he was never meant to have.

In the middle of all this I thought of the Lord's Prayer, in which we ask God to not only forgive us of our sins but also to give us the strength to forgive those who have sinned against us. And so my own journey to Colossae began every morning when I left our little apartment on the Upper West Side of Manhattan and walked across Central Park and back. Along the way I would call Jason's name and declare forgiveness in my heart for him. Some months later I began to pray prayers of blessing over Jason and his family. I cannot tell you when exactly it happened, but some years later I was surprised by the release in my heart for him. Somewhere along the way the levees of unforgiveness and bitterness had broken. I was far from Rome, but the journey was not over.

Someone once observed people only change when the pain to remain the same becomes greater than the pain to change. Imagine you really don't like going to the dentist.

It's a chore, like taking your car to the mechanic for a routine oil change where they are destined to find a greater problem. But your tooth is really hurting to the point that your mouth feels like it's on fire. No matter how much you dislike the dentist, you end up in the office because the pain of staying the same is greater than the pain of addressing the issue.

In my case, I did not want the pain associated with my unforgiveness. And I for sure did not want to ask God to deal with my sin while I prayed blessings over my betrayer. I was driven to make a change because I was awakened to the ugly truth of what my refusal to forgive was doing to me. Not only had my vulnerability and transparency dissipated, but so had my joy. These painful revelations pushed me to meet with God.

Let's imagine I never embarked on the long road back to my own Colossae by dealing with the truth of my unforgiveness. I would not be much use as a friend to anyone. Friendship demands intimacy, and how is that possible if I'm too busy holding others at a distance? People who refuse to make the long journey of change will never make good friends.

As painful as it is to be confronted with our faults, the greater pain is the decision to stay the same. What will our refusal to face the beast get us in the end? Not the joys of sustained friendship. At some point we must go to the dentist's office. Fools stay at home while their mouth is on fire. The wise get off the couch and make the appointment.

Friendships often derail due to mutual culpability. Because of this, both parties are in need of repentance. Onesimus is not the only one who has a long road to walk. Philemon has his own road as well.

7

EXCUSES

It's time to deal with the elephant in the room. We touched on it lightly when I mentioned the great Howard Thurman's grandmother, who refused to read the letter of Philemon, along with Paul's other writings, because they were (mis)used by her owners as grounds for her enslavement. Mother Thurman is hardly the only one to harbor sincere reservations about Paul's letter. Honestly, it is hard to ingest. Bible-believing abolitionists did the exact opposite of what Paul instructs Onesimus to do—they protected slaves along the underground railroad rather than send them back to their enslavers. So what gives?

For years, Bible scholars have danced around the matter by saying slavery in Rome was far different from slavery in the first few centuries of American history. No doubt their observations carry a measure of merit. Often, Roman slaves were more educated than their owners and were people of great means prior to their captivity. Many were professionals of great service to their owners. What's more, they were not enslaved because of the color of their skin. So, yes, there exist significant differences between the Roman and American approaches to slavery. But aren't we just splitting hairs? At its core, both systems' commitment to slavery was based on its very definition—the owning of people. Onesimus rightly understands the inhumanity of being the property of another.

No one articulated the inhumanity of being possessed by another quite like Frederick Douglass and Sojourner Truth, with the latter experiencing indignity and mistreatment as an enslaved woman. Sojourner Truth was once beaten so badly she had to use a cane for the rest of her life. She fought for the emancipation of all slaves as well as for the rights of women. In her most famous speech, "Ain't I a Woman?," delivered in 1851, Sojourner Truth exhaled,

> Look at me! Look at my arm. I have plowed, I have planted, and I have gathered into barns. And no man could head me. And ain't I a woman? I could work as much and eat as much as man—when I could get it— and bear the lash as well! And ain't I a woman? I have borne children and seen most of them sold into slavery, and when I cried out with a mother's grief, none but Jesus heard me. And ain't I a woman?[1]

Let's say Sojourner Truth stole from her owner to finance her escape, and the revelation of her theft was brought to the attention of a Jesus-loving abolitionist who told her she now had to go back down South to her owner to make amends. This is the exact dilemma Onesimus has in the book of Philemon. When it comes to reconciliation, there are always very good reasons as to why someone should stiffen their neck and resist. We would more than understand if Onesimus not only pushed back against Paul but also gave him a good evangelical cussing out.

While I was born much too late to be the legal property of a person in America, I have been the recipient of racism. When a classmate called me a racial epithet in my first year of college, I was devastated. No, it wasn't my first time being called such language. But the wound was especially painful because it happened at a Bible college where everyone claimed to be followers of Jesus. His words that noonday hour on campus sent me into an emotional tailspin. I felt the waters of bitterness and hate toward him and all white people rise within me.

Around this time my father visited me, and unaware of the incident, he asked me about my future plans. I told him I'd much rather drive trucks than be around white people. My words jarred him, and me. As these "feathers" left my mouth, I knew I was in sin and needed to begin the long road back to Colossae. It would take me a considerable amount of time to take my first steps back, but I finally mustered up the courage to write a letter to the person who had hurt me, asking him to forgive me for my sin of unforgiveness. I don't say these things to guilt white people or to make myself look like some hero. Hardly. But the main reason for my delay in leaving the Rome of my unforgiveness is that the flesh and the Spirit within me were embroiled in a very long back and forth. The flesh articulated more than its fair share of justifications as to why I owed no attempts at reconciliation.

Today, being counted among the oppressed is equivalent to receiving a congressional Medal of Honor. Because of this, many choose to wear oppression as an ornament and use it as an excuse to not forgive. Unforgiveness is an act of theft whereby we refuse to acknowledge the humanity of those who wronged us because we do not look the beast in the eye. While there are certain acts of cruelty and in-justice that close the door to reconciliation, we must take the first steps out of Rome nonetheless by offering for-giveness, without which reconciliation is never possible.

There will always be very good reasons as to why you should not be reconciled to certain people. Justifications abound as to why you should never sit at the table of friendship with your ex-spouse whose act of betrayal took your breath away. And why you should not make amends with the father who abandoned you.

The older I get, the more difficult friendship seems to be. I'm running out of energy to come back for yet another round of sit downs, truth encounters, and "come to Jesus" moments to do the inescapable work of friendship. Much has been made of the dissipation of sexual vitality as we age, but we don't really talk about the relational vitality needed as our emotional bandwidth recedes. Sometimes I wish there were a pill for this as well. There goes Frank, popping off at the mouth again. Let me take this friendship pill so I can get the energy needed to have yet another chat. Oh, Cheryl disregarded my feelings? Hold on, let me go to the medicine cabinet. In the absence of these pills, it's easy to shrug my shoulders and sigh to myself, *I just don't have the time to do this anymore.*

But remember, most relational breakdowns have more than one offender. I'm not the only one who would love to have a friendship pill. When both parties have the truth encounter, they are bound to bring two very different perspectives on what led to the downfall of their relationship. The dad who neglected his responsibilities at home could gently push back and say there was a lot more at play, like the demise of his relationship with the child's mother. But the problem is, children well into adulthood do not see their father's departure as merely leaving their mom but as leaving *them*. Then there are all the justifications surrounding the gap between what was done and what was intended. When confronted, the offender reaches for their version of "charge it to my head and not my heart," which is far from helpful. Or the offender suspects they have wounded the other—but because they have not been confronted, they shrug as if to say it wasn't that big of a deal, and the friendship slowly dies. And of course, there's always the offender's pride lurking beneath the surface. Even if they do see the wrong they committed, the apology just won't roll off their tongue but gets caught in traffic somewhere around their esophagus.

I grew up in one of Atlanta's southside suburbs. Even as children in the 1980s, we knew as black people to never venture into the Georgia town known as Forsyth. Their reputation for hating blacks was well documented. In 1912, two black men were wrongly accused of murder and were promptly lynched (technically executed since a sham trial was convened). What followed was a mass eviction of nearly eleven hundred blacks who were run off their property, leaving Forsyth an all-white community that remained that way for nearly the rest of the twentieth century.

In the sixties and seventies, Dr. Marcus Mashburn became the preferred doctor in Forsyth. He attended to many who had participated in the famous lynchings of 1912, describing them as being psychologically tormented as they shared their deathbed confessions with him for having participated in such injustice: "As they grew older, their minds [were] burdened by having had a part in the killing. . . . This thing, they knew, was wrong."[2] Reconciliation never occurred because these men refused to admit their wrongdoing, all while hiding behind a façade of lies and excuses.

While we might not have participated in lynchings, many of us do know the psychological torment of participating in the execution of a friendship. We can be silent, but our refusal to speak will not make things better or assuage our guilt. To this day, the town of Forsyth struggles to rise from the ashes of its past because it won't leave Rome and make things right.

Paul did not participate in the dysfunction of Philemon and Onesimus's relationship, but his perceived silence has, for many people, placed him on level ground with the racists of Forsyth. I must admit my unease with Paul's lack of forthrightness in not coming against slave-owning Philemon. But any fair reading of the letter, along with an understanding of the times, forces us to see Paul differently. He does, for example, come against slavery when he appeals to Philemon to take Onesimus back no longer as a slave but as a brother. His plea is not in the vein of emancipation but something even more audacious. Paul is after reconciliation.

If Paul has his way, Onesimus takes off with his letter in hand and heads back to Colossae in the company of his comrade Tychicus (Colossians 4:7-9). As he ventures into the Lycus Valley, his heart rate speeds up. He is close to home. He raps on the door, and Philemon appears. Before Philemon can react, Onesimus bows to his social superior and shoves the letter into his hands, imploring, "Sir, please read this. It's from Paul." So, Philemon gives it a read. Then another. And another. Maybe they turn in for the evening without a conversation.

A few days go by. Philemon shocks Onesimus by inviting him for the first time to share a meal at the table with him, his wife, Apphia, and his son, Archippus. Onesimus is stunned to receive the same allotment of food as his former master. He is treated as an equal when Philemon queries him on his trip and how Paul is doing. This is repeated at the next meal, and the next, and the next. Onesimus apologizes for stealing. Philemon reciprocates by offering his own apologies. There has been a total repatterning of their relationship. They are friends now. The master-slave dynamic is done.

If you're wondering if this has now gone from a work of nonfiction to a fairytale, know that what I have just envisioned can't be too far of a stretch. According to many leaders of the early church, Onesimus ended up becoming the bishop of Ephesus.[3] How was this possible? There's no way a slave ascends the ecclesiological ladder to bishop without first becoming a brother. And there is no way for Onesimus to go from a runaway slave to a brother without first coming to terms with why he needed to leave Rome and venture back to Colossae.

I've laughed and cried over the years when I think of the sovereign irony of God at play in my own life. To think of the number of books I've written, conferences I've spoken at, and lives I've shaped in the area of ethnic unity and racial reconciliation is indeed laughable, considering at one point I was so embittered with racial trauma I would rather drive a truck than work with a certain race of people. My "ascendancy" up my own ladder began in my little bedroom, where I put down my excuses, picked up a pen, and asked forgiveness from the one who had wounded me. That decision to leave Rome has brought me to the Colossae of my destiny.

The work of repentance and reconciliation is not so much about the relationship, as important as that is, but something far more. When we refuse to remain enslaved to our justifications and instead decide to leave Rome to go back and make things right, we are marching down not just the road of change but the road of destiny. We are headed to the place where God wants to transform us from slaves to brothers to bishops.

8

THE CALVARY WAY

I often wonder what the initial conversation between Onesimus and Philemon was like when they finally decided to broach the subject of what happened and how to move forward. Until they could venture into reconciliation, Philemon would have to kick things off because of his position in the social hierarchy. Maybe Epaphras, one of the leaders of the church who meets in Philemon's home, is brought in to mediate the conversation. The three sit down and Philemon begins, "You stole my things, and there's no way we can even discuss friendship until they are returned or restitution is made." Onesimus counters, "I never would have been in your home to take your things had you not enslaved me." Philemon interjects. Back and forth they go in a never-ending tennis match of rights, with both becoming more entrenched in their justifications.

In the journey of friendship, if I always lash out in response to the inevitable slights I receive from the other person, I will never know the joys of long-term friendship. "I will. I did" is out the door. In its place will be an inevitable loneliness where I am walled off by my own acts of retribution.

Take the legendary baseball player Ty Cobb as an example. He knew nothing of humility, only holding on to his rights. If you wronged him in any way, intentionally or not, brace yourself for his wrath. Once while playing a game in New York, Cobb had heard enough heckling from a certain fan named Claude Lueker, so he jumped into the stands and pummeled him. While he was not the first or last player to do such a thing, this was not a fair fight. Lueker was disabled: he was missing his right hand and three fingers from his left. Another time, a street worker asked Cobb to walk around the wet cement he had just poured. Offended, Cobb punched him in the face. Yet another time, Cobb assaulted a bellboy at a hotel and also got into a row with a groundskeeper and his wife. He knew nothing of the concept of repentance. Over the years his teammates pleaded with him to tone it down, but their words fell on deaf ears.

Toward the end of his life Cobb said with pride, "I am pleased to note that I didn't overlook any important punitive measures."[1] Around this same time, Cobb also sighed, "If I had my life to do all over again, I would have had more friends."[2] Cobb's assessment of the poor state of his relationships was spot on. Of all the people he played baseball with, only three showed up to his funeral. This was his just compensation for a life in which he refused to let things go.

For all his abilities, no one would ever assess Cobb as a humble person. His whole orientation to life was a "me first" disposition, and if you threatened him in any way, you paid the price. Words like *arrogance*, *pride*, and *narcissism* are apt descriptors of Cobb. So is the word *lonely*.

On the surface, it's hard for us to relate to Cobb. I'll go out on a limb and assume you've never assaulted a disabled person or punched a dude's wife in the face. But we all have our own little prideful ways of settling the score and getting even. Like Sean Connery's character says in the movie *The Untouchables* as they are about to start a war against the infamous Al Capone and his gang, "They pull a knife, you pull a gun. He sends one of yours to the hospital, you send one of his to the morgue. That's the Chicago way." This way of never letting things go is a barrier to repentance and friendship. Let's be honest, the Chicago way is embedded deep within us. We don't get the invitation, so when it's our turn to host an event, we don't send the invitation. You do something to offend me, I stop talking to you. I don't think you're treating me with the respect I deserve, I respond in kind by not giving you respect. Round and round it goes—the Chicago way.

The only way out of this is humility. While pride—this idea of independence—is the number one killer of friendship, its antithesis, humility, is the prime nourisher of healthy relationships. If Onesimus and Philemon have any hope of sitting at the table of brotherhood in a new paradigm of friendship, they have to repent. There is no such thing as repentance without humility, because to change your actions is to acknowledge you were in the wrong. Humility in every stalled relationship from Onesimus and Philemon to you and I today has several facets, with the first being confession.

Prideful people will not apologize, at least not the right way. Have you ever heard a high-profile person like a celebrity attempt an apology? It's a real head-scratcher, to say the least. Typically, some huge transgression occurs where everyone knows that person is in the wrong. After some conference with the celebrity's inner circle, the conclusion is made that they need to extend an apology. They take to social media, hold a press conference, or render a statement that says something to the effect of, "What happened is not really who I am. If anyone was hurt by my actions, I'm sorry." Cue the record scratch followed by a lengthy period of awkward silence. *That's* the apology? This scenario isn't limited to celebrities and politicians. I'm pretty sure we've been on both sides of the table here. I've had truth encounters with people who wounded me, and when we worked through it, they messed the whole thing up by saying, "Bro, I sure didn't mean to cause any harm. So if you felt harm, my bad." Not an apology. Or, "Man, that was completely out of character for me." Oh boy.

The Bible is clear that what we say and do is never dislocated from our hearts. Remember the whole horns and halos bit? We have to embrace an uncomfortable truth: both our act of generosity and our breach of integrity are who we are. We are nuanced people, and what we do flows out of our hearts, places occupied by the flesh *and* the Spirit. The gossip is who I am. The lie is who I am. God is working on me, and the journey of sanctification means I am progressively becoming more and more like Christ and less and less like the old me deeply marked by sin. When I harm you in our odyssey of friendship, humility requires me to admit the truth that the offense is who I am. I don't like it, and I want to grow past it, but I must own it first.

Derrick and I have been doing life together for almost thirty years. He's a real model to me of owning the less than pleasant aspects of one's character. Over the course of our friendship, Derrick has watched me experience some measure of success and has cheered me on. At the same time, he has confessed how hard it's been to do this given we both are pastors and how prone he is to compare the size of our churches, degrees earned, books written, and speaking engagements invited to. Derrick once confided that in his quiet moments he wrestles with envy toward me. He has asked me to pray for him. This level of vulnerability, where he owns the not so pretty aspects of his character, has only served to nourish our friendship. Humility refuses to put a filter on character.

Onesimus and Philemon do not sit at the table of brotherhood if Onesimus says, "If me taking your stuff hurt you, that's so not who I am. Sorry if you were offended." Rather, a proper apology *takes ownership* and never settles for "I'm sorry if . . ." There's no "if" at all.

A proper apology then *names the offense*: "I'm sorry I lied." "I'm sorry I slandered you." In the case of Onesimus, "I'm sorry I stole from you." Or Philemon, "I'm sorry for enslaving you."

Finally, it ends with *the big ask*. After Onesimus and Philemon both named their specific transgressions and took ownership of them, they would have concluded by asking of each other, "Will you forgive me?" It takes humility to apologize the right way, but this is the only way to go to war with the Chicago way.

To repent is to be humble, and humility is the vulnerable act of making genuine apologies whereby we take ownership, name the offense, and seek forgiveness. Humility also means we do the completely un-American thing by letting go of our rights. Our pride is so obsessed with rights it results in hands clenched so tightly they are never free to open up and give to the other. While we do have certain basic rights, like the right to be treated with dignity and respect, we must at the same time discern that much of what we hold on to are lesser items—life's sugar packages.

The way of the kingdom is not through Chicago but through Calvary, where we ease the grip on our rights and open our hands in vulnerability so we may know the joys of sustained friendship. This is what Jesus focused on in his controversial Sermon on the Mount. I say it's controversial because there are scores of interpretations to his sermon throughout church history. At the heart of the confusion is the impossibility of Jesus' message as well as the idea of his words insulting our pride. Toward the end of Matthew 5, he unleashes a frontal assault on our preoccupation with rights when he says if someone slaps us, we are to turn the other cheek. If a person sues us and takes our tunic, we are to let them have our cloak as well. And, if we are forced to go one mile, go two instead. For Americans, who have been embedded with the idea that life is about the right to liberty and the pursuit of happiness, Jesus' words rub against the very grain of how we have been culturally formed. There's just no way around it: the way of the kingdom attacks our prideful dispositions by calling us to lay down our rights.

These words of Jesus are not merely words but a life he lived. Paul reminds the Philippians that even though Jesus was God and could have exercised his rights by refusing to come to earth and be treated with such blatant inhumanity, he did the completely counterintuitive thing by dying on a cross. Sure, he could have called a legion of angels to wipe out his accusers, boarded a cloud, and returned to heaven all while we wallowed in our sins with no hope. But he did not. Jesus Christ, God in the flesh, laid down his rights by receiving what should have been our punishment. Paul concludes by naming Jesus' act as humility: "And being found in human form, he humbled himself by becoming obedient to the point of death, even death on a cross" (Philippians 2:8). The outcome of such humility is that you and I can now be reconciled to God through Christ. There is no friendship, no experience of intimacy with God, without the humble abdication of rights by our Lord and Savior, Jesus Christ. To be Christians means we must mimic this vertical humility horizontally to others.

Philemon and Onesimus have very good reasons as to why they should not apologize and seek a reimagined future as brothers. Philemon has the right to say brotherhood is off the table until restitution is made. My sympathies are weighted more toward Onesimus, who is well within his rights to say there's no way he even takes one step out of Rome toward Colossae given he was enslaved by this man. Humanly speaking, their arguments are justifiable. But within the contours of the kingdom, led by a King who modeled the act of releasing rights, they have no real excuse but to give it a go. Their pride must die, and the nail in pride's coffin is placed by the hammer of humility.

To be humble is to die. Is this not what the betrayed spouse does when she, through tears, agrees to go to war with the Chicago way by giving her adulterous husband another chance? It is death to acknowledge you were wrong and humbly ask for forgiveness with no excuses or attempts to justify your actions. And it is just as hard to turn the other cheek to the person who lied to you and open the door in deep vulnerability to a new chapter of friendship. This, friends, is death. A new and vibrant friendship can only happen when it emerges from the ashes of this kind of death. We are most like Christ when we go the way of Calvary.

When we are at death's door and inevitably stare into the rearview mirror of our lives, we will not take joy in our acts of retribution. We won't relish those moments when we held on to our rights for dear life. Instead, we will grieve over the graveyard of relationships that died far too soon because we chose the way of Chicago over the way of Calvary. We will wish we had been far more like Jesus and died to our rights.

PART THREE

GRACE

9

HESED

The ancient Celts so valued the concept of friendship they coined a term for it—*anam cara*, or soul friend. In their mind, the *anam cara* was not just someone you went to the pub with to discuss the latest sporting event, nor even someone you sat next to in church. Rather, this kind of friend was someone you shared your innermost self with in the journey to belong. To the Celts, it was unthinkable to consider yourself a follower of Jesus and try to walk the path of life alone. The *anam cara* was as essential to life as food and water.[1]

My mother has several *anam caras*. They're a handful of women who met decades ago in Atlanta when they were all young mothers trying to make sense of life and figure out what it meant to follow Jesus. They also happened to all go to the same church. I'm not sure exactly how it happened, but over time they came together and committed to one another in their own way. These ladies put a name to their bond: "the Stones." No, it's not inspired by The Rolling Stones but by a story in the Bible when God tells Joshua to set up stones of remembrance to remind Israel of his faithfulness to them (Joshua 4:1-7). These ladies were going to love God and each other so much that they would be a reminder to one another, and their children, of God's faithfulness. And that's what they have done. They meet monthly for lunches, show up when their children (and now grandchildren) get married, and walk with each other in life's inevitable valleys.

I saw this recently when my father was grieving the death of his sister. A woman came up to me to extend her heartfelt condolences. It was one of those embarrassing moments where she clearly knew who I was while I had no clue who she was but felt as if I should. After our awkward exchange, my sister whispered in my ear, "That's Maria, one of the Stones." She had driven over one hundred miles to be with my folks in one of the hardest moments of their lives. If I were a betting man, drawing on their decades of life together, I'd say they will be there for each other as each is lowered into the grave. Over the years these black women have lived out the Celtic notion of *anam cara*.

This all sounds well and good, but don't think for a moment that the Stones didn't have their problems. Over the years they experienced moments of frustration and come-to-Jesus conversations in which some of them were confronted on their sin. One threw up her hands and just gave up on the group, going years without returning anyone's calls. Soul-level friendship often feels like a full-time job with periods of bad compensation.

We all long for a small squadron of *anam caras*. The problem is not in the longing or even in the initial finding but in the maintaining because, like you, that soul friend is a sinner whose actions at some point will offend you. What then?

At some point, Philemon reads Paul's letter and is confronted by some uneasy truths, mainly to take Onesimus back no longer as a slave but as a brother. Paul's appeal transcends the legal and cultural rights afforded to Philemon. Remember, under Roman law, Philemon had the right to order Onesimus's death by crucifixion. Had Paul merely asked Philemon to let Onesimus live, that would have been a request for mercy. But Paul goes beyond mercy when he petitions Philemon to take him back as a brother. Legally, Onesimus does not deserve this. Here, Paul is making a play for something that flies at a much higher altitude than mercy and rights: grace. Everything, and I mean everything, hinges on this.

When two people fall out of sorts, they need to have a truth encounter to get to the bottom of what happened. They have to explore the self-centeredness, the lies, and the pettiness. But then the question becomes, How will they respond to the truth once it has been excavated? The offender has begun the road of repentance by apologizing and asking forgiveness. These are wonderful starts. But they still haven't arrived at reconciliation. Everything now dangles on how the offended party responds. Will they go the Chicago way or the Calvary way? Will they hold on to their rights or release them in great humility and show grace? They can do the work to arrive at truth, and the offender can apologize perfectly, but if the other person does not stop looking at the offense and refuses to extend grace, the relationship is dead. When Onesimus apologizes for his theft, in those few moments of silence as he awaits Philemon's reply, his life flashes before his eyes. In those seconds he's either headed to a literal cross or the table of brotherhood. Everything rides on the fulcrum of grace.

C. S. Lewis once happened on a conversation about what makes Christianity unique compared to other religions. He quickly interjected with a one-word response: "Grace."[2] Lewis is right. From Genesis to Revelation, the whole Bible rests on this one word, grace. It may come as a surprise to some that grace is at work in the Old Testament. I grew up in a very legalistic church where grace wasn't talked about much. When it was, it was only explained (poorly, I might add) from the New Testament vantage point, as if grace had been unemployed until Jesus arrived on the scene, but this is a fallacy.

The most important word in the Old Testament is the Hebrew word *hesed*. It is used some 250 times, with over half of those times (127) appearing in the book of Psalms. Most often, the word *hesed* is translated as "steadfast love." But to be honest, steadfast love doesn't really get at the heart of the word because it is almost impossible to define *hesed*. If the heartbeat of *hesed* has to do with the character of God in relationship with his people, then how in the world do you explain that? It's like the time I came back from Cape Town, South Africa, and my wife asked me how the trip was. I told her how beautiful Cape Town is, but when she pressed me to describe its beauty, words failed me—and I work with words for a living. Sure, I talked about Table Mountain and the coming together of the Atlantic and Indian Oceans, but my feeble attempts at articulation just didn't do the place justice. That's *hesed*.

Trying to explain *hesed* is like trying to put into words what I felt the first time I heard jazz saxophonist John Coltrane's classic *A Love Supreme*, the album he recorded after what he calls his spiritual awakening. *A Love Supreme* is, in his words, his offering to God. Words to adequately express what I felt as I listened to Coltrane fail me. That's *hesed*. Or trying to explain to my grandchildren how I felt when I was at Madison Square Garden the night Steph Curry broke the all-time three-point record. I can give some descriptors, but words don't come close to capturing the atmosphere, the joy, and the exhilaration we experienced when the ball went into the hoop, making him the greatest three-point shooter ever. These are mere illustrations, shadows of a much greater entity—God. If I struggle to put into words the beauty of Cape Town and the transcendence of Coltrane and Curry, how in the world can I describe God's kindness toward us? Now you see the dilemma with *hesed*.

The best explanation I've seen for *hesed* is from musician and author Michael Card. In his book *Inexpressible*, he describes *hesed* as "when the person from whom I have a right to expect nothing gives me everything."[3] If grace means to give to someone something they do not deserve, then the Old Testament equivalent of grace is *hesed*. In a sense, this is exactly what Paul is asking Philemon to give to Onesimus.

Throughout the Bible we catch vivid pictures of *hesed*. Not long after God miraculously delivers the nation of Israel from Egypt, they do the unthinkable by worshiping an idol. God calls Moses in for a closed-door discussion in which he pretty much says it's time to do a hard reset. God plans to wipe out all of Israel and start fresh with Moses, who by this time is well into his eighties—but hey, Abraham was in his nineties when he and his wife had their first child together, so this is nothing for God, right? Moses pleads with God to show *hesed* to Israel. Yes, because of their idolatry, Israel has no right to expect anything from God, but will God give them everything by continuing to lead them into the Promised Land? In a

moving scene, God affirms his commitment to extend
grace when he shows his glory to Moses and declares,
"The LORD, the LORD, a God merciful and gracious, slow to
anger, and abounding in *steadfast love* and faithfulness,
keeping *steadfast love* for thousands, forgiving iniquity
and transgression and sin" (Exodus 34:6-7, emphasis
mine). Do you see it? In this list of attributes, God chooses
twice to describe himself as being full of *steadfast love*,
or *hesed*. Again, he is saying that while Israel deserves
nothing, he will give them everything.

Or take the story of Hosea and Gomer. Frustrated with
Israel's idolatry, God says he wants Hosea to marry a pros-
titute. Is God being punitive in demanding that this man
of God get hitched to a woman of the night? No. Hosea's
marriage is to be an illustration of God's *hesed* with adulterous Israel. In Hosea 3, when Gomer cheats on Hosea,
God tells him that even though he has the right to divorce
her, he must go get her, which he does. Gomer has no right
to expect anything, but Hosea gives her everything. This
is exactly how God deals with Israel.

What about the story Jesus tells of the youngest son who
asks for his share of the inheritance early? Wounded by his
son's words, the father relents and watches as his son
hurries out the door for the far country where he wastes
his money on immorality. Finally, with no money left, he
returns home hoping to convince his father to take him
back no longer as a son but as a servant. When the father

sees his son, he runs to greet him. The young man launches into his speech, full of shame. "Nonsense," the father interjects. "You're my son. Kill the fattened calf. Bring out the best robe and ring. Call the DJ, and let's Cupid Shuffle all night." (I think that's the idea of the Greek translation!) The son has no right to expect anything, but the father gives him everything. That, friends, is *hesed*.

Of course, the ultimate image of *hesed* in the Bible is the cross. We have worshiped our own idols of success, status, money, relationships, and possessions. We have lied, slandered, gossiped, and acted jealous and envious. We have no right to expect anything from God given the ways we have offended him. Yet the message of the cross is that as far as the east is from the west is how far God has removed our sins from us. The cross says God has way more mercy than we have mess. The cross is the place where earning ends and grace begins, because we are not some hired servants thinking we can pay off our debt. Just as the father welcomed his broke, immoral son, Jesus says to us, "You're my son. Call the DJ and let's have a party. Welcome home!" We have no right to expect anything, but because of what Jesus has done on the cross, we get everything. Our whole faith and our relationship with God rest on *hesed*.

Do you see it? The Bible depicts grace not so much from an ideological vantage point but from a relational one. God with Israel. Hosea with Gomer. A father with his youngest son. God with us through Jesus on the cross. And if Paul has his way, Philemon with Onesimus. Grace was never ultimately meant to be the name of a school or a church or a doctrinal category, but a lived reality, flowing through the offended toward the offender. Grace nourishes and sustains friendship.

In June 1996, a white supremacy rally was held in Ann Arbor, Michigan. Keshia Thomas, an eighteen-year-old black high school student, was there with a group of African Americans to protest the rally when someone shouted that a member of the Ku Klux Klan (KKK) was among them. While tensions were already high, they now escalated to a fever pitch. The other blacks were ready to pummel this young member of the Klan, who had a Nazi tattoo and was wearing a shirt emblazoned with the Confederate flag. The young man fell to the ground. Sensing he was in danger, Keshia Thomas jumped on top of him to shield him from the protestors' attacks. The image of a black woman protecting a white Klansman became one of *Life* magazine's pictures of the year in 1996. It's hard to forget pictures of grace.

I look at that picture often, and I always wonder what that young man was thinking as he was being protected by the very one he had been taught to hate. I then wonder what happened to him once the danger subsided and the rally ended. I bet you he changed. Whatever preconceptions he may have held about black people probably ended that day, because that's what *hesed* does—it changes you. He had no right to expect anything from Keshia, but he got everything.

Paul, in asking Philemon to show grace to Onesimus, reminds him that he, too, has received grace: "If he has wronged you at all, or owes you anything, charge that to my account. I, Paul, write this with my own hand: I will repay it—to say nothing of your owing me even your own self" (Philemon 18-19). What does Paul mean when he says Philemon owes him his "own self"? This can only be a reference to Paul leading Philemon to faith in Christ, at which point he experienced the *hesed* of God. Having received such *hesed*, Philemon is now being asked to extend this grace to Onesimus.

An ungracious Christian is an oxymoron, a contradiction in terms. The picture of Keshia protecting a member of the KKK offends me as a black man, until I see it in light of the cross. Then I realize I'm not Keshia—I'm the man being covered. Daily I offend God. Daily I insult God. Daily I play the rebel. I have no right to expect anything from God, yet daily I receive everything. To be a Christian means I extend grace to those who have wronged me, leaving open the possibility of friendship.

10

THE FULCRUM OF GRACE

To extend grace is to suffer. Philemon finds himself in this position when he reads Paul's letter asking him to forgive the debt Onesimus has incurred. This means Philemon will never recover the possessions taken from him. Maybe they were jewels or something else of high monetary value. Maybe he had planned to bequeath them to his son Archippus and any other children he might have, but just like that, his plans and his possessions went out the door. For Philemon to take Paul's words to heart—to give everything to someone who has no right to expect anything—is costly.

Lest you think I'm being hyperbolic when I equate grace with suffering, look to the cross. Philemon's motivation to part with his possessions and never seek restitution is exactly what happened on Calvary's hill when Jesus died for you and me. Our debt did not simply vanish but was placed on the shoulders of the Man of Sorrows, who felt God's wrath in the graceful act of propitiation. As the hymnwriter George Bennard said, the old, rugged cross is indeed the "emblem of suffering and shame,"[1] yet at the same time there is no picture of grace more profound. On that Friday grace and suffering merged, and the same holds true for you and me. To offer grace is to suffer because it cuts against the grain of our flesh and its desire to get even.

I once was invited to preach at a seminary where one of the premier preachers and preaching professors in all the world, Dr. Robert Smith Jr., was in the audience. To say I was nervous was a gross understatement, but I made it through. Later that day, I found myself seated on an airplane across the aisle from this professor I adored. We struck up a conversation that spanned from my pleas for him to help me improve as a communicator of God's Word to one of the most painful episodes of his life. Some years earlier, Dr. Smith's son had been murdered. A cloud of grief hovered over him and his wife. Parents are not supposed to bury children, and with the suddenness of this heinous act, there was no time to prepare and say goodbye. Just like that, their son was gone.

Months later, a grieving Dr. Smith felt compelled to visit his son's murderer in jail. While he didn't give me any details of their visit, it must have been awkward as they sat talking on phones on either side of a glass partition. The visit soon ended, followed by another and another.

Over time an unlikely friendship began to emerge between the killer and the father of the deceased. Eventually, Dr. Smith shared the good news of Christ with his son's assailant. Like Paul with Onesimus, he became this man's father in the faith. As the newborn Christ-follower began to grow in his walk, he confided to Dr. Smith that while he knew he was not getting out of prison, he felt called to preach the gospel in jail and seriously study the Bible. Soon after, money was raised to fund a scholarship named after Dr. Smith's deceased son. The first recipient of this scholarship was the man who killed him.

I could not believe what I was hearing. Who does this? Think of the cost involved and the kind of suffering Dr. Smith endured along the way when he chose to violate his fleshly proclivities of vengeance and instead chose to bless the very man who had gutted him and his wife.

This process happened over a long period of time. Dr. Smith did not wake up the morning after the murder with a grand plan to share the gospel with his son's killer, much less offer to pay for his education. Like the journey of repentance, arriving at a place where grace can be extended takes time. Dr. Smith would have been well within his rights to never visit in the first place and instead just privately confess to God that it was beyond his capacity to sit with a person like this. We more than understand this. We would also understand if Philemon chose to stop short of having Onesimus turned in to the

Roman authorities for execution. Mercy would have been enough, right? Yet where is the gospel witness if Dr. Smith never went to the prison, or if Keshia Thomas simply looked on while the KKK member received his just due, or if Philemon stopped short of both the cross and the table of brotherhood?

Grace insults our sensibilities because it is irrational. You and I live in a meritocracy, a world that says we earn what we deserve. The athlete understands this more than anyone else. Make enough tackles, catch enough touchdowns, hit enough home runs, and they will be recruited to the right college, drafted into the ranks of the professionals, and rewarded with riches. The student gets this, too. Study hard, show up, make the right grades, and they will go to the right college, get hired by a great company, and be compensated well. The meritocracy is so woven into the fabric of our culture that any attempt to explain it is like trying to describe water to a fish. We only come to terms with the pervasive nature of the meritocracy when we make the great grades and don't get into the college of our dreams, or when we work hard but find ourselves unemployed. Nothing jars us out of our moral senses like when the meritocratic equation does not work out.

This is everything when we think about friendship. I was disappointed with Howard, the friend who would not "play tennis" with me, because I felt as if my altruistic acts of friendship had placed him in my debt. When the equation didn't work out, when he didn't respond as I felt he should, I realized my altruism was anything but. Friendship is not like the workplace, where if I feel mistreated I can simply appeal to the human resource department or file a suit to get what I think I deserve. What to do with the friend who doesn't return the invitation, the call, and the acts of kindness? Or what to do in the case of the spouse whose husband took off to Vegas on the day he retired and in one weekend spent their entire life savings at the casino, only to come back empty and have to beg for his job back? (True story, by the way.)

This then brings another question to mind: How far does grace go? Would it be ungracious for Dr. Smith to not set up the scholarship, for Keshia to not cover the KKK member, or for the wife whose husband wasted their retirement to leave the marriage? God is infinite; he has no limits. But we do.

In the Bible, grace is a junk drawer filled with different items. When Jesus tells us to love our enemies—to show kindness to people who have no right to expect anything—that's grace. When we are commanded to forgive, to literally send the offense away, that too is in the junk drawer of grace along with many other things. Where do we draw the line when it comes to grace? That's a complicated question. We are obligated to forgive, so grace must always be dispensed on those who are in our moral debt. Jesus did say we are to forgive seventy times seven. He's using hyperbole, and his point is that forgiveness—an act of grace—should have no expiration or statute of limitations. There is another kind of grace, which goes further than forgiveness and seeks to repair the relationship so the two can venture into their reimagined future. This kind of grace does have limits.

We have a very limited view of grace—we think of it as flowing in one direction from the person who has been offended to the offender, from Philemon to Onesimus (though, as we have said, Philemon bears culpability as well). But giving grace makes no difference within the context of a relationship if it is not received.

Let's say Philemon does what Paul appeals to him to do. Not only does he lay down his right to kill him, but he receives him as a brother. Then some weeks later, Philemon discovers Onesimus has stolen from him again and again and again. There comes a point where there is no hope for reconciliation, not because grace was withheld but because grace was never received. We know a person has received grace because grace changes them.

This is the epicenter of Victor Hugo's classic tale *Les Misérables*. What happens to the hardened criminal Jean Valjean when he is caught taking off with the bishop's possessions? When Valjean is captured by the police, all the bishop would have to do is say, "Yep, that's my stuff. He's a thief," and off he would go back to prison. But that's not what happens. In an unbelievable act of grace (all grace is unbelievable because it goes against the meritocracy), the bishop lets him off the hook, and he's free. This one act changes Valjean's life. He's no longer a hardened criminal but a man who cares for the marginalized and shows deep compassion, even to the person who is relentless in his pursuit to destroy him.

It's one thing to give grace, quite another to receive it. How far do we go with giving grace? When the person chooses to resist the gift, the relationship cannot proceed. How do we know if they have received grace? If there is a softening, along with a commitment to venture out of Rome and walk the path of repentance, then grace has been received.

This is why Paul is both hopeful and bold in his plea for the former slave and master to become brothers. Philemon and Onesimus have each received the grace of God as followers of Christ. When they had no right to expect anything, God gave them everything. Have you ever wondered why so much of the Bible centers around instructions in our relationships with others? Why does Jesus say an unforgiving Christian is an oxymoron, or a greedy Christian who never does anything for the poor is likewise an oxymoron? Why are we so insulted by Jesus' words in his Sermon on the Mount to turn the other cheek and love our enemies? Because the only real way we know we have received the grace of God is that it gives us a whole new orientation in how we relate to others. If we want to discern what Philemon believes about the gospel, we have to look at how he deals with someone who has stolen from and wronged him. This is why community with people for the long haul can be so hard: they draw us out and lay us bare, exposing what we really believe about the gospel and grace.

As our children enter adulthood, I find myself a bit disoriented. This is the natural course of things as I realize I no longer have the control I thought I had (if ever at all), but also because I am in the vulnerable position of reaching for their grace as I reflect on the many mistakes I made when they were in our home. I've come to realize that if we are to have any chance at an authentic, vibrant friendship—sitting at the table together as more than father and son but as brothers—I will need their grace. So far they have been more than kind, and I am gaining confidence with the inaugural steps we are taking in this new season.

I can speak similarly of my relationship with my mother-in-law. Boy, did we get off to a rough start. Today, however, we have a beautiful friendship that began on a note of grace when she helped us get out of financial debt. Now that she is in her retirement years, we are blessed to help her in many little ways. We reformed our relationship by both extending and receiving grace, and even suffering a bit along the way. Now, we sit at the Thanksgiving and

Christmas tables together and enjoy many visits and phone calls in between, full of joy in each other's presence.

I also keep coming back to the table with my friend Howard, who by his own admission is a far better responder than initiator. Over the years I have said things that cut him deeply and acted in ways that make me blush. Howard grew up poor and has struggled financially well into his adult years, which means any talk of money is a sore spot for him. Once without thinking, I offered Howard unsolicited financial advice, which triggered him. When his anger subsided, I asked for his forgiveness, and he extended grace. Our friendship continues to this day because of grace.

Every friendship I've ever had has either died or thrived on the fulcrum of grace. Far too many times, I chose the way of the meritocracy and cut friendships short because the other person did not do their part. Other times I refused to genuinely receive grace, thinking I was above what was being offered. As I look back on these dearly departed friendships, I feel deep remorse over my insistence to refuse grace. May we all become people who both receive and extend grace to others.

11

USELESS TO USEFUL

There comes a point in an athlete's life when the gig is up. The moment their skills inevitably begin to diminish, they are shown the door. This is the way the meritocracy works. When Steph Curry comes to the negotiations table, the people on the other side will not consider his joyful spirit or stable home life as a significant factor in whether he gets a new contract. Ultimately what matters is what he can produce. Sports can function as a meritocracy because they have a reduced view of humanity. This is the same in the business world: hit your numbers for the quarter and you will get the bonus, but miss them and you could find yourself out of a job. Grace doesn't thrive in environments where people have devolved into numbers.

We are best positioned to offer and receive grace when those we are in relationship with value the fullness of our humanity. Paul knew this, which is why he makes a seemingly offhand comment to Philemon: "(Formerly [Onesimus] was useless to you, but now he is indeed useful to you and to me)" (Philemon 11). I call Paul's words "offhand" because his passing remarks are in parentheses in the English Standard Version of the Bible. I don't know about you, but when I come across words in parentheses, I whiz right on by. But we miss a crucial point Paul is making if we choose to ignore these words.

The name *Onesimus*, which means "useful," was common for slaves in Paul's time. It's an inhumane name because it relegates the person to the status of an instrument of productivity. When the Puritan pastor Cotton Mather was negotiating his compensation package at a church he interviewed with, he made it clear a slave was to be provided. The church acquiesced, and he named the slave "Onesimus" and referred to him as "It." To Mather and a myriad of other slave masters throughout history, their property was not human but a tool. This is why black women were first called "hoes" in the antebellum South—they plowed fields with this instrument and were seen as mere objects of productivity.

There probably came a point when Philemon accepted the reality that Onesimus had taken off with his possessions, never to be found again. Philemon probably shrugged dismissively and said, "Oh well, didn't need him anyway. He's useless to me now." Onesimus, as his name suggests, was only in Philemon's life to service him. When he no longer hung around to offer his services, the relationship was over.

Let's not be too hard on Philemon. If we are honest with ourselves, a bit of his spirit lives in us. I'm shocked at how easy it is for me to be condescending to a server, barista, or flight attendant. I have to refer to them as such because I don't know their names. They exist in my life only to provide a service, and when they are reduced to this level, it's easy to snap at them and mutter, "Useless."

To some degree, we can understand the transactional nature of our interactions with people in the service industry. The trouble comes when we relate to people in this way under the guise of friendship. Aristotle pointed this out in his "Friendship Ladder"—sometimes we have the propensity to cozy up to people solely for pleasure or utilitarian means. When we do this, we become like Philemon and regard the other as useless when they fail to measure up to our expectations.

Anyone who has ever watched the television series *The Fresh Prince of Bel-Air* will tell you the most impactful episode was the one where Will's estranged father pops back into his life and promises to take him on a trip.[1] The day of the journey arrives, but Will's dad cannot go through with it. He's gotten an opportunity to make more money, so he up and leaves. When Will finds out, he reacts at first with nonchalance. *I didn't need him anyway*, he reasons. *I'll figure life out on my own and be successful.* But soon the emotions start pouring out of him. "To hell with him!" he screams.

There are many reasons we find ourselves moved viscerally by Will's reaction. On one hand his father has become the villain, and rightfully so. Who would exchange time with their own son for a little extra side work? In a way, the father is saying to his son what he has said practically his whole life: "Useless." But on the other hand, Will is branding his dad useless as well. Until they both peel these labels off, there will be no hope for a relationship.

The name calling continues today. Many go to divorce court calling their soon-to-be ex-spouse useless. When the revelation of our friend's betrayal surfaces, we respond by naming them useless. When we try over and over again to find a church community where we can bear our souls and be nourished in our faith, only to come up empty again and again, we label the whole project useless and retreat inward. When we have given ourselves to see racial healing, only to be wounded by insensitivity or ignored in the midst of our hurt, we throw our hands in the air and call the whole thing useless. In all of these instances and more, we will never know the joys of sustained relationships if we allow ourselves to whisper, "Useless."

Racism, sexism, classism, gang activity, and our current divisive political climate continue because we have looked across the divide and called the other side useless. Until we throw this label away and see all people as intrinsically valuable, we will never know true unity. I'm certain this is why Sojourner Truth's speech "Ain't I a Woman?" was so profound: she demanded people acknowledge not only her gender but, more importantly, her intrinsic worth as a fellow image bearer. Her words are a plea for people to throw away the *useless* label because she knew she would never be treated as an equal until people turned the corner from useless to useful.

This is Paul's message to Philemon. All hopes of reconciliation are out the door as long as Philemon sees Onesimus as useless. Paul not only reminds Philemon of Onesimus's name—he's useful—but in a stroke of genius, he also declares that Onesimus's worth is not limited to Philemon's home where he is nothing more than a servant. Slave or free, in Colossae or Rome, Onesimus is of inestimable value because he is a child of God and now a brother in Christ.

Paul situates Onesimus's value not in his actions but in his being. He is someone who Jesus stretched out his hands and died for. This unsettles me because I can't evade the gospel's harrowing truth—Jesus died for the lynched and the lynch mob, the faithful spouse and the philandering one, the friend who kept the confidence and the one who betrayed the confidence.

But there's more. While Paul explicitly says (albeit in an offhand, parenthetical way) that Onesimus is useful, he focuses on Onesimus's inestimable worth throughout his correspondence with Philemon. Notice again the language of family that Paul employs. He refers to Philemon as a brother—which I would do well to remember as a black man with all my temptations to cancel slave-owning Philemon. As a brother, he is a member of God's family who I will spend eternity with. Paul continues this familial language when he refers to Onesimus as his child in the faith and urges Philemon to receive him as a brother. By referring to Onesimus as his child, Paul postures himself as a spiritual father. These three make an unlikely family—a slave owner, a thief, and a murderer. Because of the gospel, Onesimus is useful not only because Christ died for him but also because he, like Philemon and Paul, has been adopted into the family of God.

Of course, there is no drama like family drama, and there are many instances in which family members fall out of sorts with each other. But it's equally true that seeing each other as family motivates us to extend grace to one another, which is Paul's point.

I learned this early on in my life. I was about eight years old when I detected tension between my father and his sister. Around the same time every month, she would call the house asking for money because she could not afford the rent on her apartment. My father would express frustration, ask a few questions, and inevitably send her the money. Once, I remember him hitting the roof when he found out she had taken his assistance and gone on a cruise. But without fail, he kept giving to her what she did not deserve.

Many years later she died, and we attended her funeral. I will never forget my father standing by her casket laughing and crying. It was a strange sight. I had to know what this was about. "She got me again," my father said through tears and laughter. "What do you mean?" I asked. He said, "Who do you think paid for this?" I cracked a smile.

I'm sure my father crossed the line from help to enablement. My aunt may have received her brother's money, but she surely did not receive his grace because it did not change her. But all of this aside, Dad kept extending grace. As he once said, "What am I going to do, let them throw my sister out on the street?" While her landlord and the world may have seen a useless woman who could not get it together, my father saw her as family, which only punctuated her value.

One of the quickest ways to destroy any friendship is to otherize and then eulogize the other person as useless. This is the way of the meritocracy. The way of grace begins with the acknowledgment that Christ died for them and sees them as infinitely valuable. The way of grace says we are family, adopted by God's grace—and family keeps coming back to the table because we see each other as useful.

12

WHAT IF?

At no point in world history has friendship been more of a challenge than now. Dr. Jeffrey A. Hall is a professor of communication studies and director of the Relationships and Technology Lab at the University of Kansas in Lawrence. He points out how data compiled over the last thirty years reveals that time spent talking to people inside and outside of the home has been in decline, and telephone and video calls have not made up for the loss. We live, Dr. Hall writes, in a "climate of interiority," where we often see people as barriers to our own personal happiness and well-being. The result has been decreasing levels of empathy and a refusal to see things from others' points of view. A cursory glance at our political and racial climate with its stark polarization proves Hall right.[1]

Our culture indeed is in the midst of a massive shift from sociality to interiority. We are becoming more withdrawn. I see this in my own life. I once confessed to my wife, Korie, that it feels as if my stamina to do the hard work of friendship has diminished. People can be exhausting. But there's way more. One of the drawbacks of technology is it gives us the illusion of relationships by keeping us a click away from old high school and college buddies, people we went to various churches with, former and current coworkers, and so on. While we may have an interaction here and there, let's not kid ourselves into thinking these are truly our friends. We do not have the capacity to have the deep, thick kind of connectivity true friendship requires with so many people.

Social media, while beneficial, can also create an illusion where we become the star of our own reality show. Someone says something we don't like? Thank God for the block button. We will create an echo chamber where we present only the aspects of ourselves we want people to see and handcraft an audience of cheerleaders who applaud our every post. Residing in a social media world where we are in control atrophies our grit and resilience muscles. So when one of our real friends challenges us, we become quick to cancel, naming them toxic and joining the hordes in our culture who retreat into interiority. None of this is what Paul nor the writers of Scripture had in mind about friendship.

Onesimus goes on to become the bishop of Ephesus. His journey from a slave to a brother to a bishop began by being challenged by Paul. Instead of hitting the block button, he responded to truth by doing the hard work of repentance. In the end, his life was bettered as he entered God's destiny for his life. But what if Onesimus had canceled Paul, tucked tail, and run? What if he had withdrawn into himself while calling Paul toxic? I bet you he would never have known the level of satisfaction and even *happiness* that comes from doing hard things. When we look at the choices of turning inward versus doing the hard work of friendship, there really is no comparison.

Early on in my ministry I had the opportunity to sit with pastors I deeply respected. I would always ask them a short list of questions, one of which was, "What are your regrets?" They all responded similarly with some version of "I wish I would have spent more time with family." I find it interesting that if you speak to any person in the winter years of their lives, all their woulda coulda shouldas are relational in nature. Or to say it another way, the older people get, the more they value people over productivity.

As with Onesimus's odyssey from slave to bishop, God has a call on your life. Psalm 139:14 points out we are "fearfully and wonderfully made." Ephesians 2:10 says we are God's work of art. You have been made on purpose and for a purpose. Your parents may not have planned on you being here, but God did, and he has good plans for you (Jeremiah 29:11). As much as we should settle into these truths, we must also reject the myth of the self-made person. I would never have gotten to where I am had it not been for people like my parents, my godfather Bishop Ulmer, and a few friends who have made a treaty with me to do everything they can to get me to where God wants me. The chronology of Onesimus's journey to becoming a bishop first required him to sit at the table of brotherhood. In the same way, we don't make it into God's desired will for our lives without sitting at the table of friendship. Resist the temptation to cut people off and turn inward. You need people far more than you know. Your destiny hangs in the balance.

But there's so much more to friendship than meets the eye. Biblical scholar N. T. Wright poses a question about the book of Philemon: What if Paul's letter were the only book in all the New Testament? All the other twenty-six books are gone. No Gospels on the life of Jesus. No book of Acts to leave us stunned at the activities of the early church. No book of Romans with its towering truths on salvation. No book of Revelation to debate over. What if?

Wright says, "If the only document we had from early Christianity was this letter to Philemon, we could deduce a very great deal about what Christianity was from this letter alone. Because we know what happened to slaves in the ancient world. And what is going on in this letter by contrast is just radically different."[2]

If the letter to Philemon were the only book in the New Testament, there would obviously be some major things missing, but there would still be enough to make us lean

in at its peculiarities. An incarcerated man asks a wealthy
slave owner to show mercy and grace to a fugitive slave by
receiving him as a brother, thus undermining the master/
slave dynamic? Such a request would violate the Roman
caste system and make any reader raise both eyebrows.
Even more intriguing is this whole business of the gospel.
What does Paul mean when he refers to Onesimus as his
child or when he, a man sitting in jail, says to Philemon he
owes him his very life? There has to be something more
going on here.

In a way, Paul's letter to Philemon is not ultimately about
friendship but about the gospel. The former is merely il-
lustrative of the latter. Paul understood something we
diminish—nothing illumines our witness and stands more
in contradistinction to our world than when we fight to
remain at the table of friendship with people who we have
wronged and who have wronged us. Put another way, my
marriage is not ultimately about my marriage but is an illustration to the world of the power of the gospel to love
when my wife and I have wronged each other. Your
friendship is not ultimately about your friendship. There's
far more at play than your happiness and enjoyment. The
world needs to see people doing life across the economic,
race, gender, culture, and eccentricity divides.

In my book *The Offensive Church*, I write of the time
civil rights leader John Lewis stepped off a bus in Rock
Hill, South Carolina. The year was 1961, and Lewis was

part of an interracial group of young people known as the "Freedom Riders" seeking to integrate bus terminals all throughout the South. His feet had barely touched the ground when he was assaulted by a white man named Elwin Wilson. Instead of fighting back, Lewis remembered his training in nonviolence and responded in resignation, giving up his rights.

In the years to come, Elwin was haunted by the image of Lewis actively loving him while he received his blows. In the aftermath, Elwin became a follower of Jesus. Almost fifty years later he reached out to Lewis, like Onesimus was charged to do, and apologized. Lewis readily extended forgiveness, and then the unthinkable happened—the two spent the winter years of their lives together conducting workshops on reconciliation. The image of the former offender and the offended, seated at the table of brotherhood, astonished and moved thousands.[3] What drove this impeccable picture of friendship was the gospel, the same impetus Paul relied on when he instructed Onesimus to go back and when he encouraged Philemon to receive Onesimus by an act of grace. Friendship done right is empowered by the gospel of Jesus Christ.

You might feel overwhelmed when you hear stories of Keshia Thomas, John Lewis, and Philemon and Onesimus, thinking, *I don't have the capacity to love like that.* That's right, we don't. And yes, I'll say it again: we need to erect healthy boundaries when people refuse to repent or receive grace. We understand this. But the gospel makes up for the difference. When our capacity runs out, the gospel rushes in. We are all Elwin Wilson, people whose sins assaulted our Lord and Savior. Yet Christ readily extends grace and forgiveness to us daily.

Our friendships are not ultimately about our joy, happiness, or fulfillment; these are mere byproducts. Rather, when we do the work of friendship by demonstrating truth, repentance, and grace on repeat, our gospel witness to the world is enhanced.

What are the particulars of this work of friendship on a granular level? In my own journey of friendship, I have found five things to be of help.

Remember when I shared the decision I made on my fortieth birthday to scale a different mountain than productivity? Well, that's the first step I have found to be tremendously helpful. It's the step of *intention*. I understand the organic nature of friendships, which tend to begin with a spark of affinity, but affinity is not enough to sustain relationship over the long haul. We need to be intentional. For me, this has meant taking the initiative to extend myself to a group of friends by calling regularly and being vulnerable with my struggles.

I also have chosen to *limit my circle* of true friends. This was really hard for me. By nature I am a connector. I cannot tell you how many times my wife has rolled her eyes when I complain about too many people having my cell phone number only to give it out again and again. So I experienced a lot of angst when I concluded I had exceeded my relational capacity. I can't do life in a meaningful way with all of the people I would love to do life with. It's just not humanly possible. This doesn't mean I cut people off, but it does mean I have to limit and prioritize. There are only a handful of people I will get on an airplane for to celebrate milestone birthdays, visit when going through seasons of loss, or confront when I see them making bad decisions. Those outside the circle get heartfelt prayers and authentic empathy, but not more. If I jumped at every opportunity to celebrate or grieve with people, I would never know the joy of thick community.

Third, I *put a name* to the friendship or have what's known in dating circles as a "DTR—define the relationship" moment. I don't suggest doing this the first few times you hang out with someone, but there does come a time when you should talk about what you're both going after. The first time my circle of friends got together for our annual retreat, Allen said, "So, what are we doing here? Each of us has a lot going on, and it's obvious we care about each other because we spent a lot of money to come to this resort. I just want to know, what are we doing?" Allen's question led to one of the most sacred moments in my life, as we spent the next few days sharing our hearts and expectations. We didn't come up with a name like my mother's group "the Stones," but we did make a treaty of sorts with each other. Since then we've met annually, connected quarterly over video chats, and call each other constantly to check in and pray.

Fourth, I've had to learn to say, *"It's okay."* There will be people who say they are in it for the long haul, but over time it just doesn't work out. Maybe they are not at a place in their emotional or spiritual maturity where they are ready to do the work of enduring friendship. Maybe they just slowly disconnect over time. I've had this happen to me, and it can lead to deep frustration. For my group's annual retreat, I found myself in recent years pleading with one friend in particular to come. Every year it was another excuse. The last time we were planning for the retreat, I remember thinking he was going to try to back out again. I braced myself for another series of conversations where I would make my best sales pitch as to why he should come. Right then, I heard a voice say, "You're not responsible. He's a grown man. If he wants this, he'll figure it out." He chose not to come, and since then he's slowly drifted away. And I've learned to be okay with it.

Finally, *friendships require investment.* People come with a cost. At times there are financial costs for things like retreats, birthday celebrations, extending financial relief in seasons of difficulty, and so on. But there's also a cost when it comes to time and the emotional and spiritual energy expended. All this and more is why our circle of enduring friends should be small. When I run the cost-benefit analysis of my circle of friends, I'll admit I sometimes experience fatigue and loss. But at the end of the day, I am a rich man because of the people God has placed in my life and the very intentional investments we have made in each other.

EPILOGUE

The Best Man **movie and television franchise** centers around a group of friends, most of whom have been doing life together since college. One of these friends is a man named Harper, who the whole series is named after because of his role as best man at one of their weddings. Like all of us Harper is complicated, an amalgamation of good and bad. On one hand he is driven, as he pushes his comrades to reach deep inside themselves to achieve their goals. Harper also has a pleasant demeanor and can be full of joy. But there's another, darker side to him. He's exceedingly selfish such that his lust for success infringes on the rights of others in his orbit. He writes a book divulging details about his friends' personal lives without asking for their permission. He buys a home his wife clearly did not want. And along the way, he proves himself to be a master manipulator so that the ends justify the means.

On their odyssey of community, Harper's friends roll up their sleeves and commit to speaking uncomfortable truths as they point out his narcissism. Throughout the series we catch flashes of contrition and repentance on his part. When shown the error of his ways he apologizes, at times even begging for a second chance. In just about every instance his friends show him grace and hit the reset button on their relationship.

No one has to deal with Harper's self-obsession quite like his wife does. Throughout the course of their relationship, she does everything in her power to facilitate his dreams while tabling hers. Finally—spoiler alert—she's had enough and divorces him, taking their only child away from him. Harper is devastated as he crashes on the sofa, alone in his home. He must be replaying the many times his friends implored him to get outside of himself and think of his wife.

Deep in the darkness of his own mind and home, the doorbell rings. It's his friends. One by one they come inside without saying much. One sets up the card table. Another pours the drinks. The other friend lays out the food and turns on some old school Earth, Wind & Fire. Harper takes it all in from his sofa as his three friends take their seats around the card table. Getting ready to deal the cards, one of them says in a muted, matter-of-fact way, "We need a fourth."

This invitation is for far more than a card game. It's a profound extension of grace. It's their own way of saying, "Not on our watch. You will make it. We are responsible for you." As middle-aged Harper pulls himself off the couch and takes his seat around the table, he's in a familiar place—one as familiar as the card tables during their college and young adult years. But this familiar place is so much more than a card game. It's similar to the table I imagine Philemon and Onesimus convened around. It's a table of friendship.

I fought back tears the first time I took this scene in, because there's a place deep within me that will forever long for this. My guess is that this is your longing as well. To fumble, to be challenged, to try again, all while being gracefully embraced ... only to fumble and try again within a community that refuses to let go. That is what enduring friendship is all about.

Yes, people can be maddening. Their besetting sins and eccentricities can drive us bonkers. But the person on the other side of the table is not the only one with issues. At various times we all are Harper—alone on the sofa, enmeshed in the misery of our own bad choices. In these moments we need a cohort of true friends who come into our home, set up the card table, pour some drinks, turn on good music, and say matter-of-factly, "Hey, we need a fourth." And there will be other times when we are the friend whose sole job is to set up the table and invite someone back into the arms of community.

ACKNOWLEDGMENTS

This book was birthed out of a series of sermons on the book of Philemon that I preached at The Summit Church in the late spring and early summer of 2021. The response to these messages was more than kind—it felt prophetic, as if the people were inviting me to broaden the circle of hearers. Their encouragement led me to spill my thoughts onto paper. I am grateful for my church. They have been a supportive family and some of the kindest people I have met. Their encouragement and perseverance with me have been a balm to my soul.

When I sat down to write this book, I didn't have a contract. When I was finished, I gave it to my agent, Andrew Wolgemuth, and asked if we could do something with it. As always, Andrew was kind and supportive, convinced this work needed to be shared. It found a landing spot with Al Hsu and my friends at IVP. This is our second book together, and I am grateful for the partnership.

There are plenty of times the acknowledgment section gives a tip of the hat to the various libraries and universities that made it possible to gain access to much sought-after material, without which the book would have been impossible. My "libraries and universities" are the many people I have come across in my travels and the circle of friends who have put up with me over the years. I refer to them by pseudonyms in this book for obvious reasons. I came into many of these friendships at a very elementary level, but over time I feel as if I have gained graduate degrees in my own growth and maturity because of their investment in me. You know who you are. I am indebted to you, sincerely.

And of course, there is my best friend, Korie. We have been married for decades now and are at the stage of life when the last child has left the nest, at least as of this writing. Most evenings we are in our quiet home, eating dinner at a table that once occupied five. We travel often together and do spontaneous things, like deciding at the last moment to go to the local jazz club or mill about one of the last remaining bookstores in downtown Durham. We still have much to say to each other, and for that I am grateful.

NOTES

INTRODUCTION: FROM "I WILL" TO "I DID"

[1]Arthur C. Brooks, *From Strength to Strength: Finding Success, Happiness, and Deep Purpose in the Second Half of Life* (New York: Portfolio/Penguin, 2022), 130.

[2]Brooks, *From Strength to Strength*, 112.

[3]Sherry Turkle, *Alone Together: Why We Expect More from Technology and Less from Each Other* (New York: Basic Books, 2012), 1.

[4]Greg Lukianoff and Jonathan Haidt, *The Coddling of the American Mind* (New York: Penguin Press, 2018), 193.

1. WHY FRIENDSHIPS ARE SO HARD

[1]Walter Isaacson, *Einstein: His Life and Universe* (New York: Simon & Schuster, 2008), 185-86.

[2]Madeline Holcombe, "Why Most Men Don't Have Enough Close Friends," CNN, November 29, 2022, www.cnn.com/2022/11/29/health/men-friendships-wellness/index.html.

2. CULTIVATING FRIENDSHIP

[1]Peter Brown, *Augustine of Hippo* (Oakland: University of California Press, 2013), 196.

[2]Brown, *Augustine of Hippo*, 57.

4. RISKY TRUTH

[1]Desmond Tutu, *No Future Without Forgiveness* (New York: Image, 2009), chap. 2, Kindle.

7. EXCUSES

[1]Sojourner Truth, "Ain't I a Woman?," in Pete Greig, *How to Hear God* (Grand Rapids, MI: Zondervan, 2022), 29.

[2]Patrick Phillips, *Blood at the Root: A Racial Cleansing in America* (New York: W. W. Norton & Company, 2016), 97.

[3]Lorne A. McCune and Derek R. Brown, *The Lexham Bible Dictionary* (Bellingham, WA: Lexham Press, 2016).

8. THE CALVARY WAY

[1]Joe Posnanski, *The Baseball 100* (New York: Avid Reader Press, 2021), 730-31.

[2]*Baseball*, "8th Inning: A Whole New Ballgame," directed by Ken Burns, written by Geoffrey C. Ward and Ken Burns, aired September 27, 1994, PBS.

9. HESED

[1]Pete Grieg, *How to Hear God* (Grand Rapids, MI: Zondervan, 2022) 203-4.

[2]Philip Yancey, *What's So Amazing About Grace?* (Grand Rapids, MI: Zondervan, 2002), 45.

[3]Michael Card, *Inexpressible: Hesed and the Mystery of God's Lovingkindness* (Downers Grove, IL: InterVarsity Press, 2018), 5.

10. THE FULCRUM OF GRACE

[1]George Bennard, "The Old Rugged Cross," 1912.

11. USELESS TO USEFUL

[1]*The Fresh Prince of Bel-Air*, season 4, episode 24, "Papa's Got a Brand New Excuse," written by Benny Medina, Jeff Pollack, and

Andy Borowitz, directed by Shelley Jensen, aired May 9, 1994, on NBC.

12. WHAT IF?

[1]Jeffrey A. Hall, "The Price We Pay for Being Less Social," *Wall Street Journal*, August 11, 2022, www.wsj.com/articles/price -we-pay-for-being-less-social-11660068416.

[2]N. T. Wright, from a pastor's retreat at St. Mary's Cathedral, Newcastle upon Tyne, "NT Wright on Philemon: 'Think Christianly,'" YouTube, posted July 12, 2015, www.youtube.com/watch?v =jESqfjqPMHE.

[3]Bryan C. Loritts, *The Offensive Church* (Downers Grove, IL: InterVarsity Press, 2023), 31-32.

ABOUT THE AUTHOR

BRYAN C. LORITTS (DMin, Liberty University) is the teaching pastor at The Summit Church, along with serving as the vice president for regions for the Send Network, the church planting arm of the SBC, where he is responsible for training church planters in multiethnic church planting. He cofounded Fellowship Memphis in 2003 and serves as president of The Kainos Movement, an organization committed to seeing the multiethnic church become the new normal.

His ministry takes him across the globe annually as he speaks at conferences, churches, and retreats. Bryan has been a featured speaker for Catalyst and the Global Leadership Summit. He serves on the board of Biola University and is an adjunct professor at Grimke Seminary. His books include *Insider Outsider*; *A Cross-Shaped Gospel*; *Right Color, Wrong Culture*; and *The Offensive Church*, among many others. He is the husband of Korie and the father of Quentin, Myles, and Jaden.

https://bryanloritts.com

𝕏 DrLoritts

⊙ @loritts

⑥ DrBryanLoritts

Podcast: *Kainos: Seeking the Multiethnic Church*, https://podcasts.apple.com/us/podcast/kainos-seeking-themultiethnic-church-with-dr/id1595620088

ALSO BY THE AUTHOR

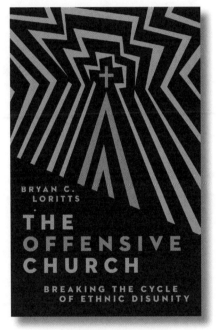

The Offensive Church
978-1-5140-0597-2